Toscana

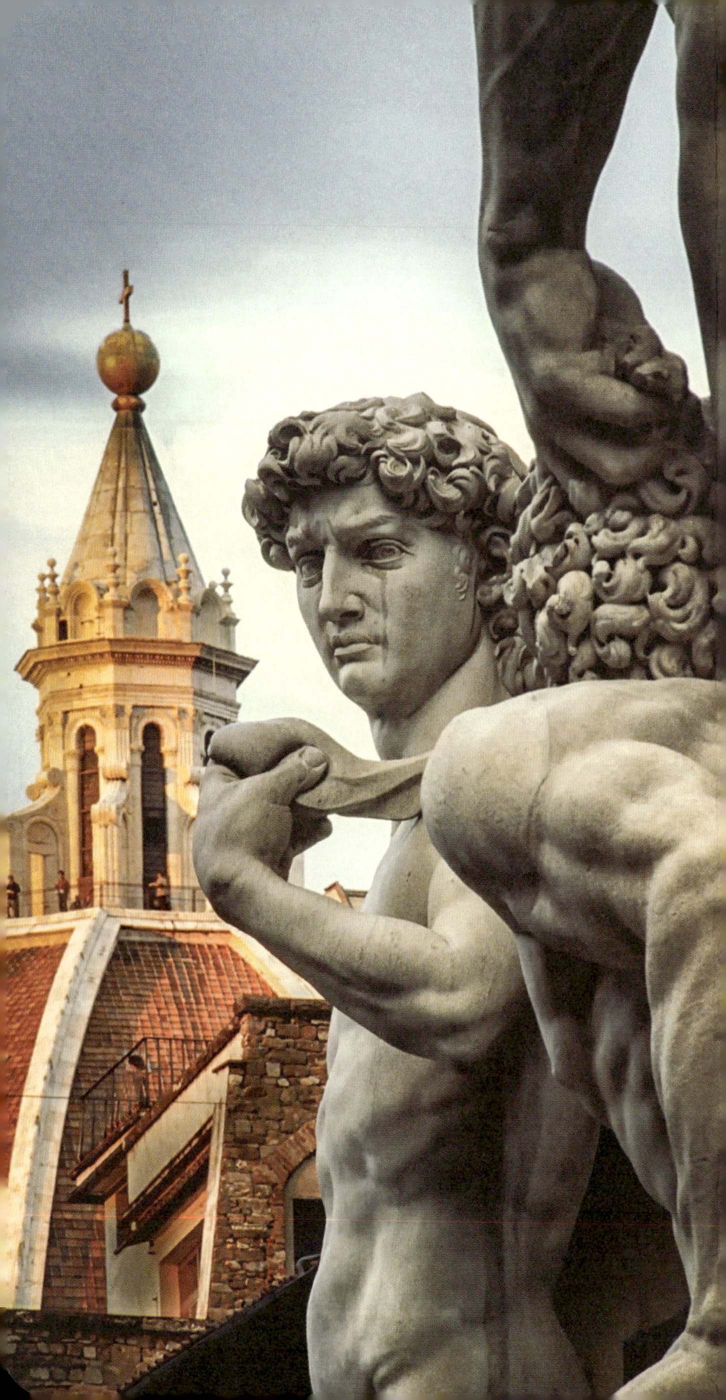

1

Il David e il "Cupolone"

Nel 1504 una volta presentato il David alla città, Firenze si pose il problema del posizionamento della statua. Eravamo nel periodo della Seconda Repubblica e il David assumeva un significato simbolico: la Giovane Repubblica avrebbe sconfitto gli iniqui potenti come David fece con Golia... Fu subito chiaro che la collocazione prevista sui contrafforti absidali del Duomo non era adatta. Si aprì un dibattito cittadino e venne istituita una commissione per indagare sul da farsi. Ne facevano parte i maggiori artisti dell'epoca: il Botticelli, Filippino Lippi, Leonardo da Vinci, il Perugino, Giuliano da Sangallo, Andrea della Robbia. Alla fine si decise per la proposta di Filippino Lippi, collocando nobilmente la statua accanto all'ingresso di Palazzo Vecchio. Questa decisione ha permesso per oltre cinque secoli di racchiudere con uno sguardo i due più importanti simboli di Firenze: Il David ed il Cupolone.

* See end pages for German and English translation

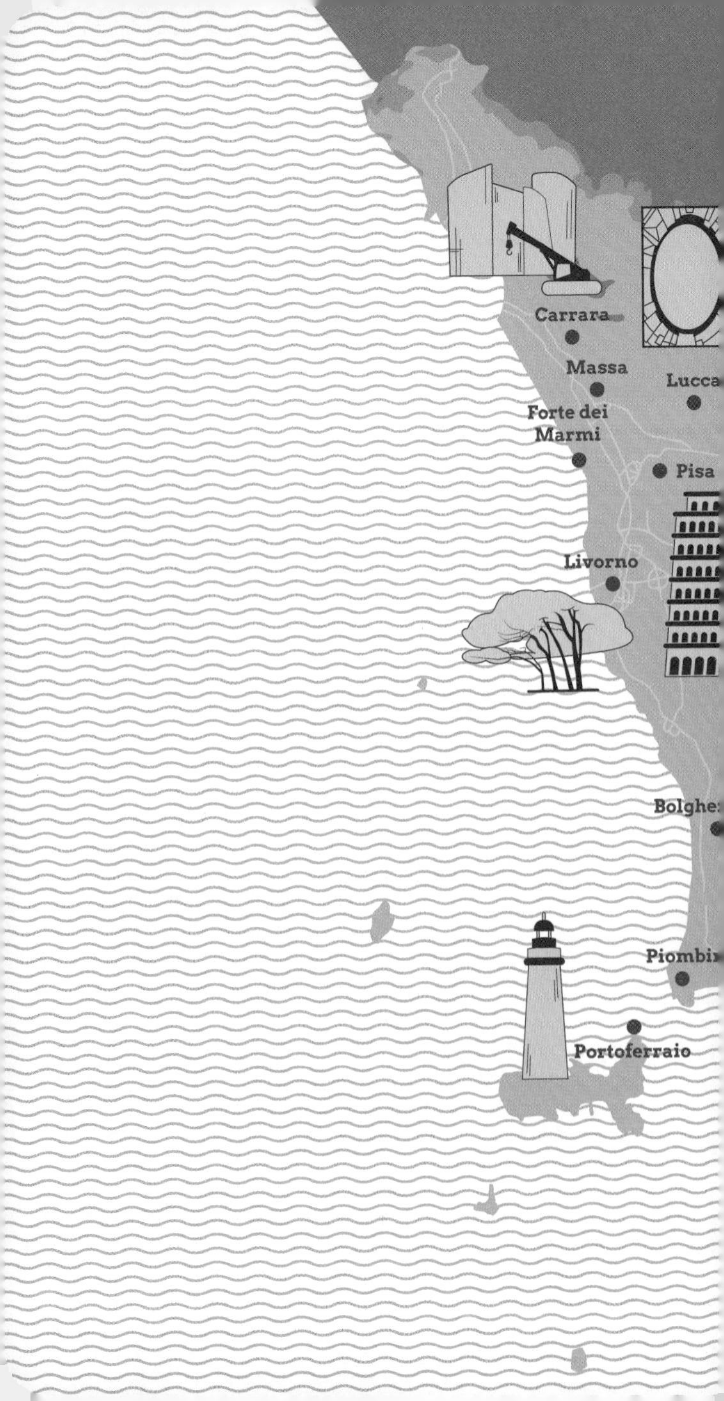

Carrara
Massa
Lucca
Forte dei Marmi
Pisa
Livorno
Portoferraio

Toscana

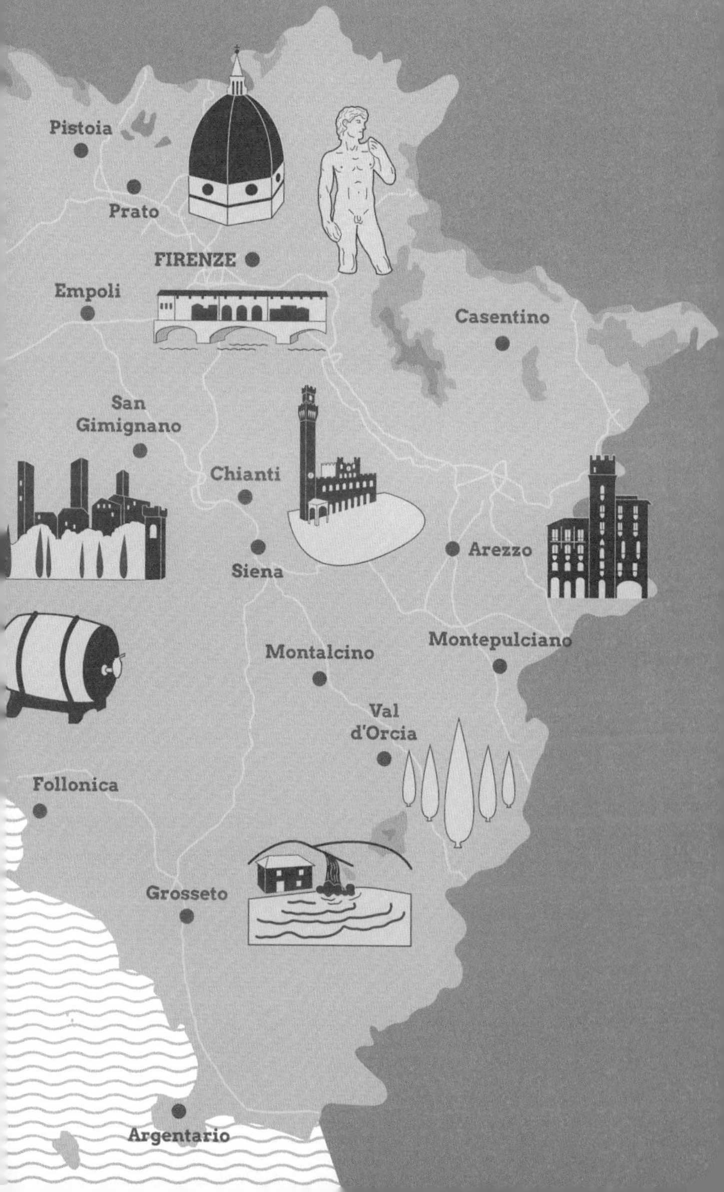

Pistoia
Prato
FIRENZE
Empoli
Casentino
San Gimignano
Chianti
Siena
Arezzo
Montepulciano
Montalcino
Val d'Orcia
Follonica
Grosseto
Argentario

2

Il Ponte Vecchio a Firenze

A Firenze si dice che ne abbia viste di cotte e di crude. Fra il 3 e il 4 agosto del 1944 i nazisti in ritirata distruggono tutti i ponti della città, escluso Ponte Vecchio. Il console tedesco Gerhard Wolf riesce a impedirne la distruzione facendo leva sul fascino esercitato dal ponte fiorentino su Adolf Hitler durante la sua visita a Firenze nel 1938. Il 4 novembre 1966 l'ennesima alluvione travolge la città, la più violenta di sempre. Ponte Vecchio sembra un fuscello in balìa delle acque dell'Arno, che superano gli archi ribassati ed inondano i pianterreni delle botteghe; ne esce malconcio, sporco, sbertucciato, le botteghe distrutte, gli alberi portati dalla piena incastrati dappertutto, ma ancora in piedi: nasce definitivamente il mito del Ponte Vecchio come ponte indistruttibile.

* See end pages for German and English translation

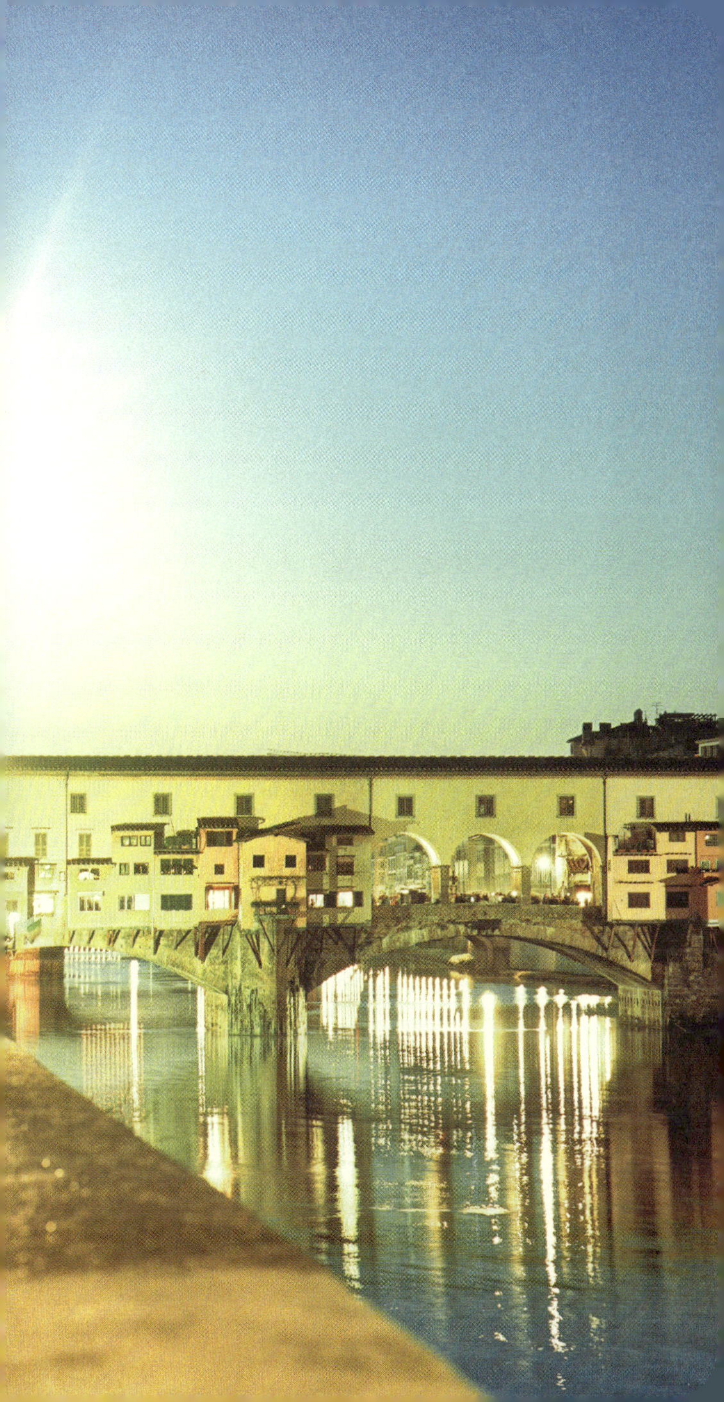

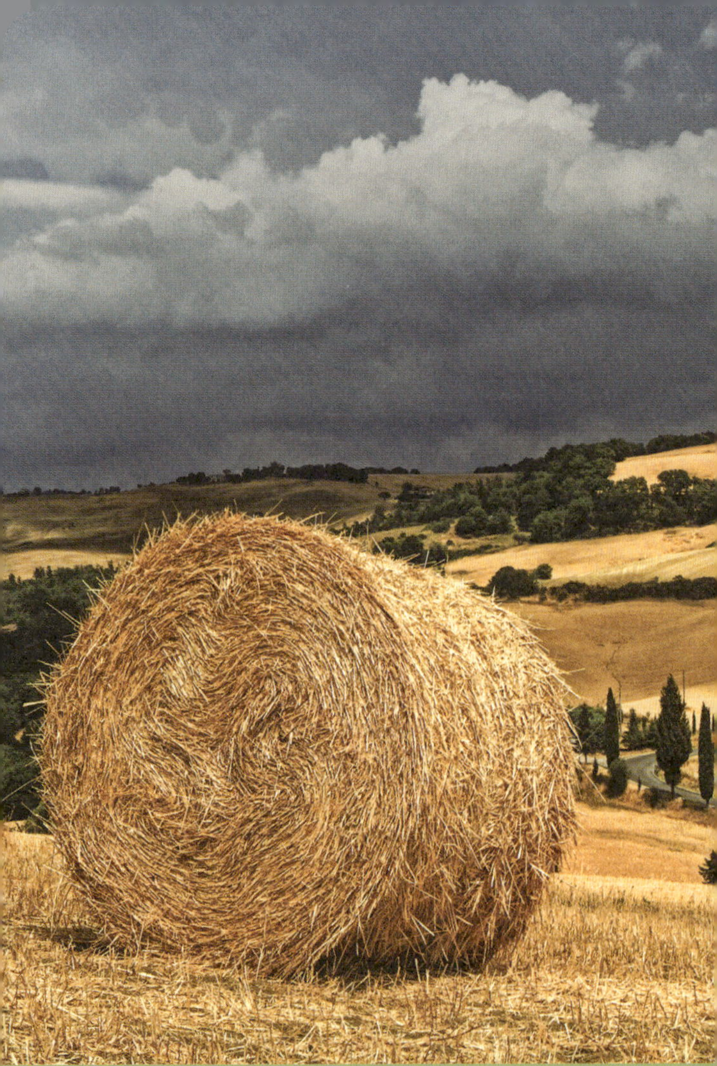

3

I cipressi di Monticchiello

Si sa, la Toscana è terra di olivi, vigne e cipressi.

I cipressi segnano il paesaggio profondamente: la natura o una mano divina li ha posti proprio lì, proprio dove dovrebbero essere. Esattamente come succede a Monticchiello.

* See end pages for German and English translation

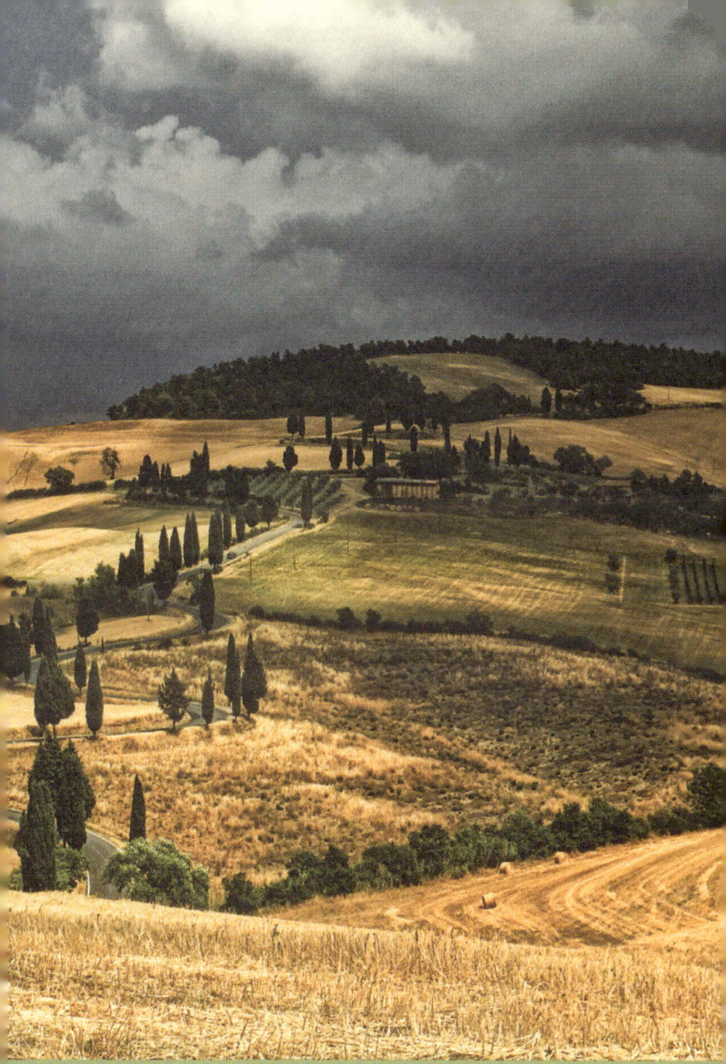

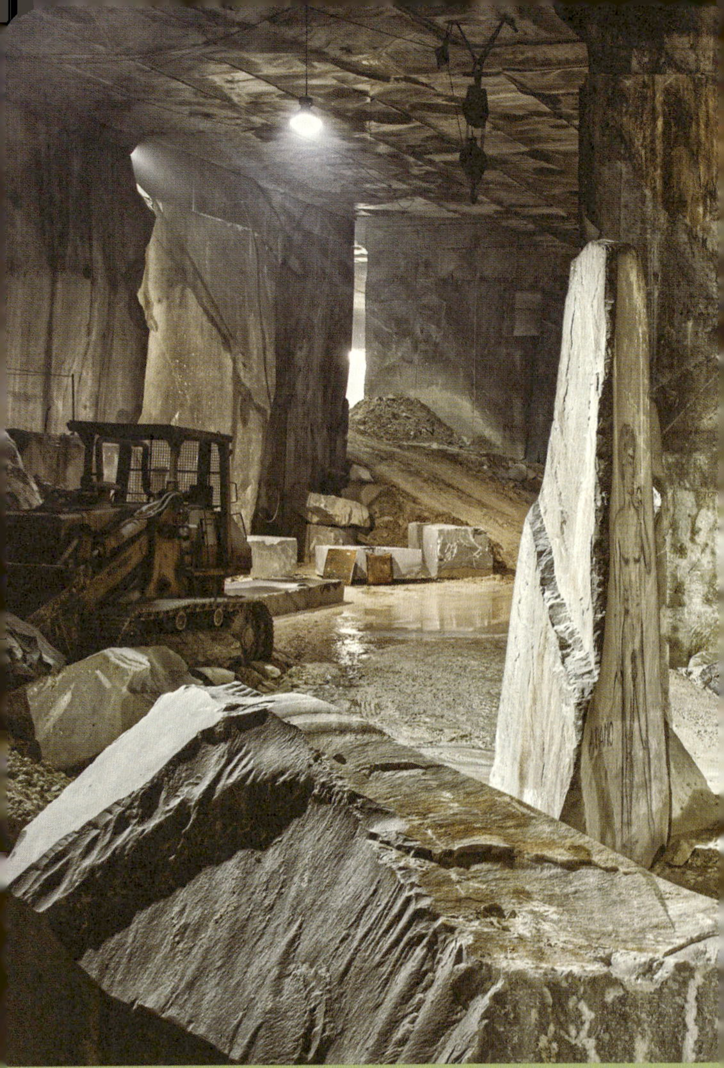

4

Cava Ravaccione n. 84

A detta di molti scultori, fra Ravaccione e Fantiscritti si è sempre cavato un Marmo di Carrara di ottima qualità. Le cave, fin dall'epoca romana, sono sempre state a cielo aperto e nei secoli hanno fortemente connotato il paesaggio delle Alpi Apuane. Nel 1963 ci fu una svolta nella tradizione, Carlo Dell'Amico inventò la tecnica dell'escavazione

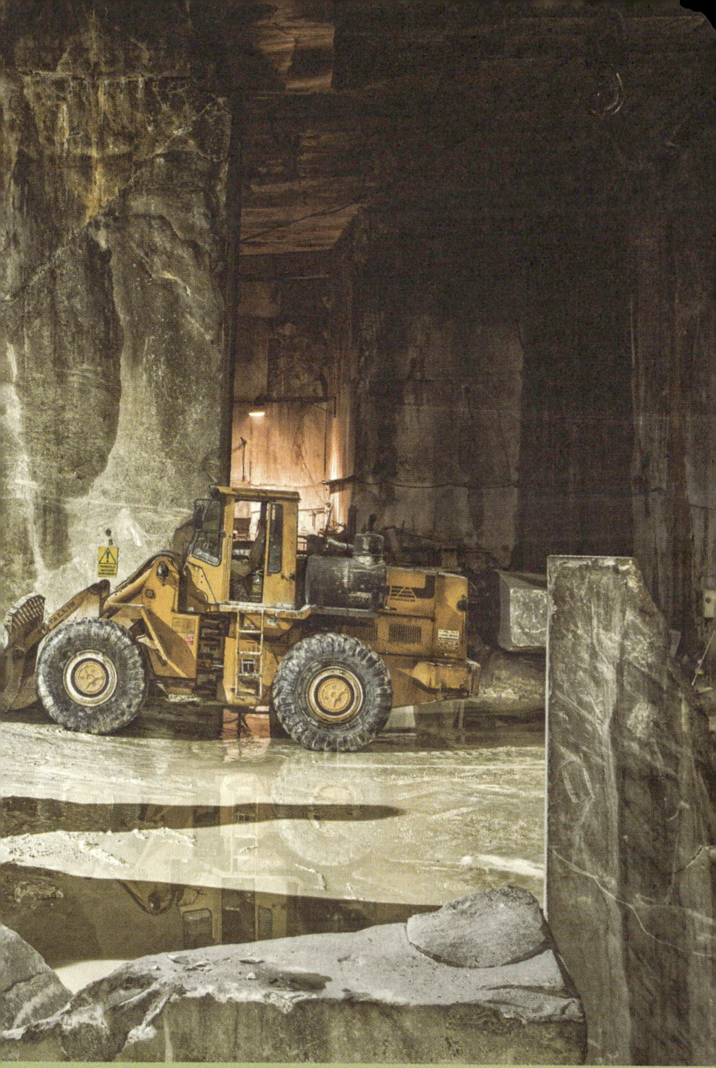

interna. Partendo dal tunnel della Marmifera, una ferrovia in disuso che serviva a trasportare il marmo, ha scavato gigantesche cavità di 24000 metri cubi sostenute da pilastri, immense cattedrali luccicanti dove si perde il senso del tempo e delle proporzioni.

* See end pages for German and English translation

5

Via Fillungo a Lucca

A Lucca è impossibile non incrociare Via Fillungo. Anche per caso ci si passa. Lunga 700 metri traversa la città dalla medievale Porta dei Borghi a Via Santa Croce, sfiora Piazza dell'Anfiteatro e la Chiesa di San Frediano. Nell'ultima parte - la parte che ricalca il cardo romano - vi si incontrano la Chiesa di San Cristoforo e la Torre delle Ore, dove, salendo, potreste incontrare il fantasma di Lucida Mansi che vendette l'anima al diavolo per rimanere giovane e bella per trent'anni. Scaduto il termine salì sulla torre per fermare l'orologio e l'incedere del tempo. Chiaramente non ci riuscì e dovette pagare pegno.

* See end pages for German and English translation

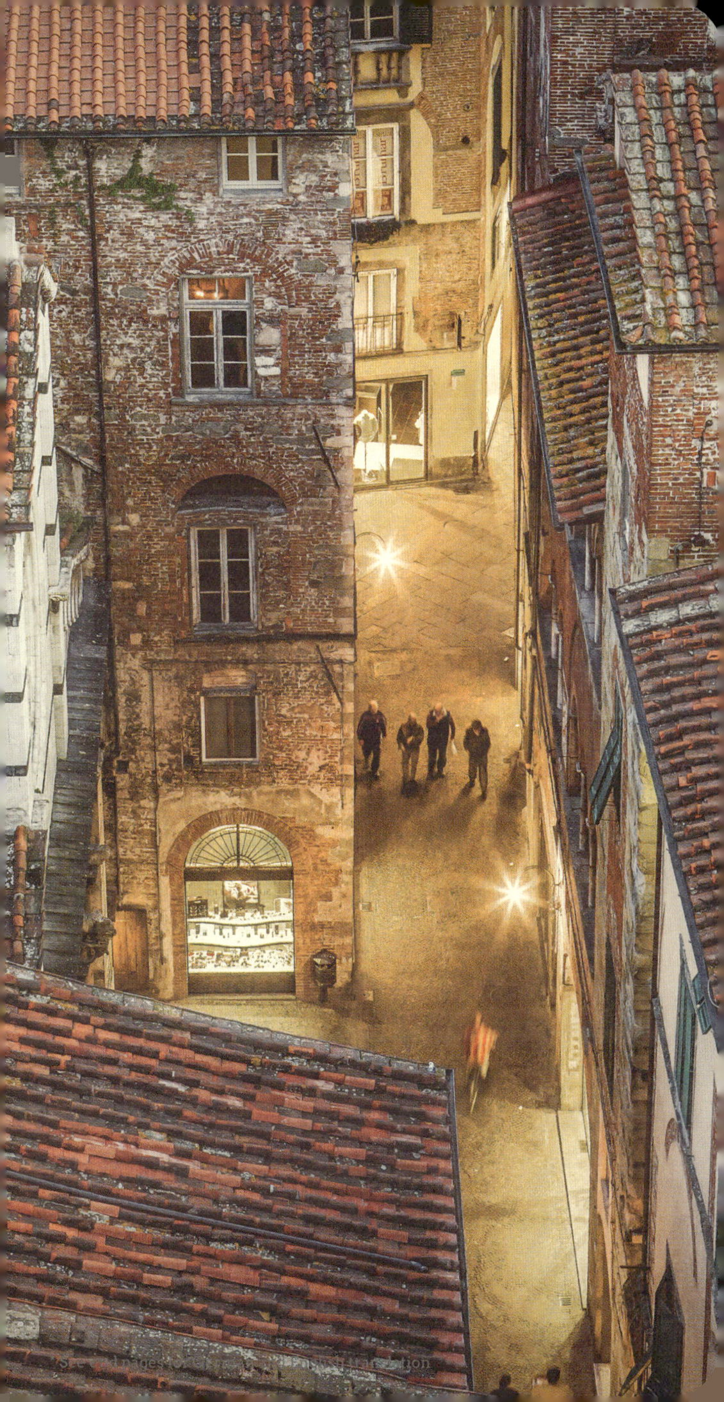

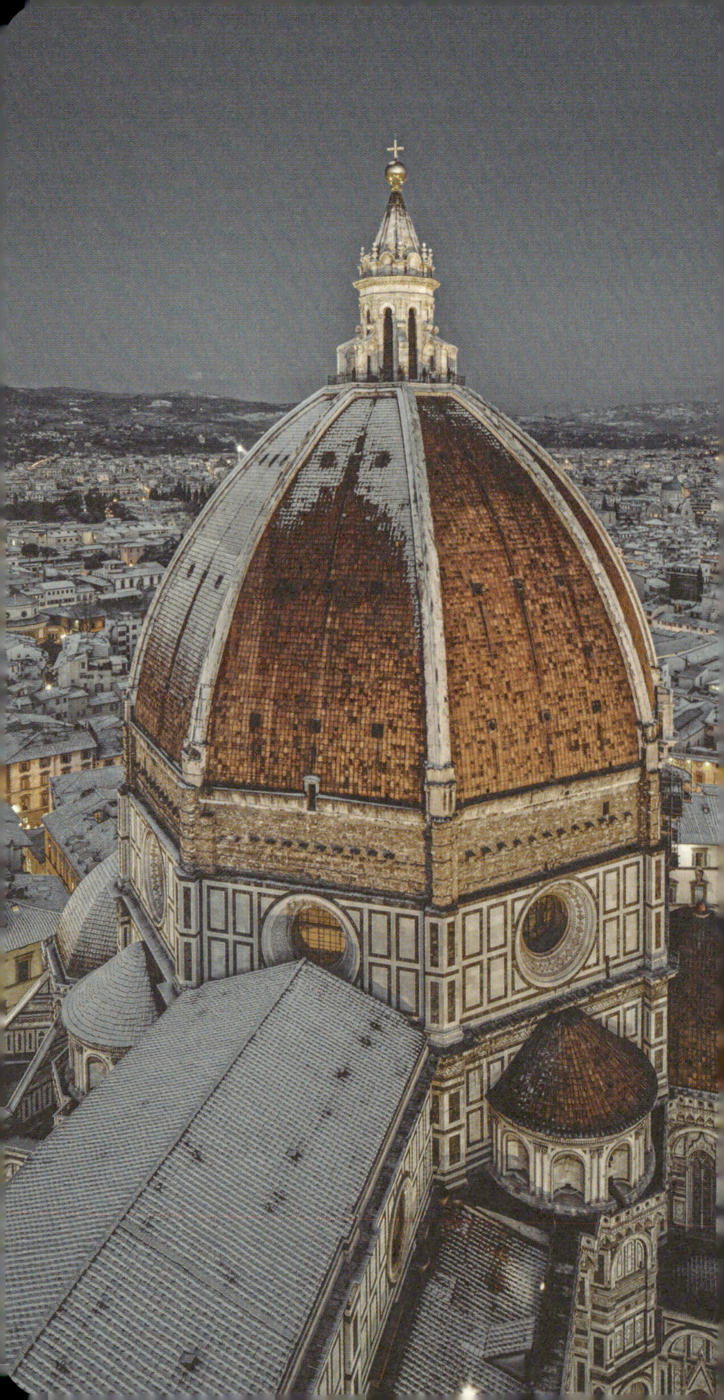

6

La Cupola del Brunelleschi

Messer Filippo si trovò di fronte un tamburo largo 77 braccia a panno fiorentine - 45 metri - e alto circa 55 metri, che doveva essere coperto con una cupola. Semplicemente doveva essere costruita la cupola più grande del mondo. Brunelleschi fu beffeggiato a lungo e additato come "somaro" dai fiorentini per aver presentato un progetto così innovativo che sfiorava l'incredibile. Niente armature e centine in legno - non avrebbero retto l'enorme peso della Cupola e sarebbero costate una follia - ma una tecnica di muratura autoportante basata sui mattoni posti a "spina di pesce" che formano due calotte concentriche. Sembra che i mattoni venissero cotti nel cantiere e avessero forma irregolare in modo da dare la giusta inclinazione alla muratura e poter "chiudere" la cupola. La Cattedrale di Santa Maria del Fiore fu consacrata nel 1436 ancora priva della lanterna: ad oggi "il Cupolone" rimane la più grande cupola del mondo costruita in calce e mattoni.

* See end pages for German and English translation

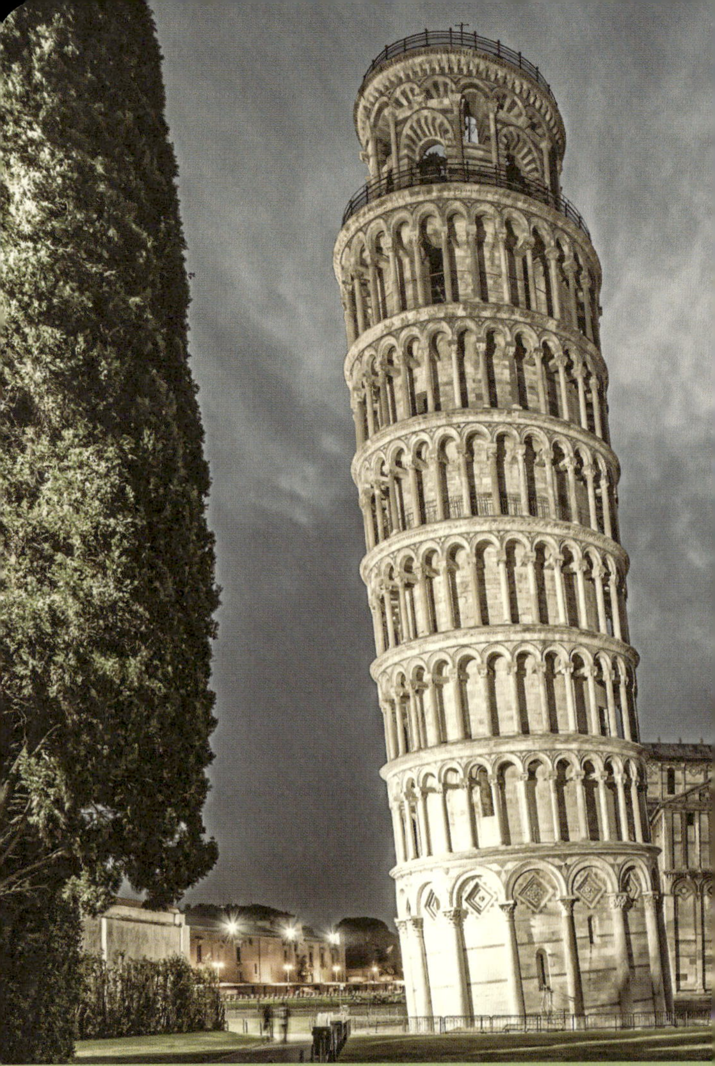

7

La Torre di Pisa

Uno dei monumenti simbolo dell'Italia nel mondo. La caratteristica pendenza è stata allo stesso tempo il suo tormento e la sua fortuna ed ha conferito a Piazza dei Miracoli qualcosa di unico. Cominciò a pendere durante la costruzione, quando si arrivò al terzo anello. Da allora nei

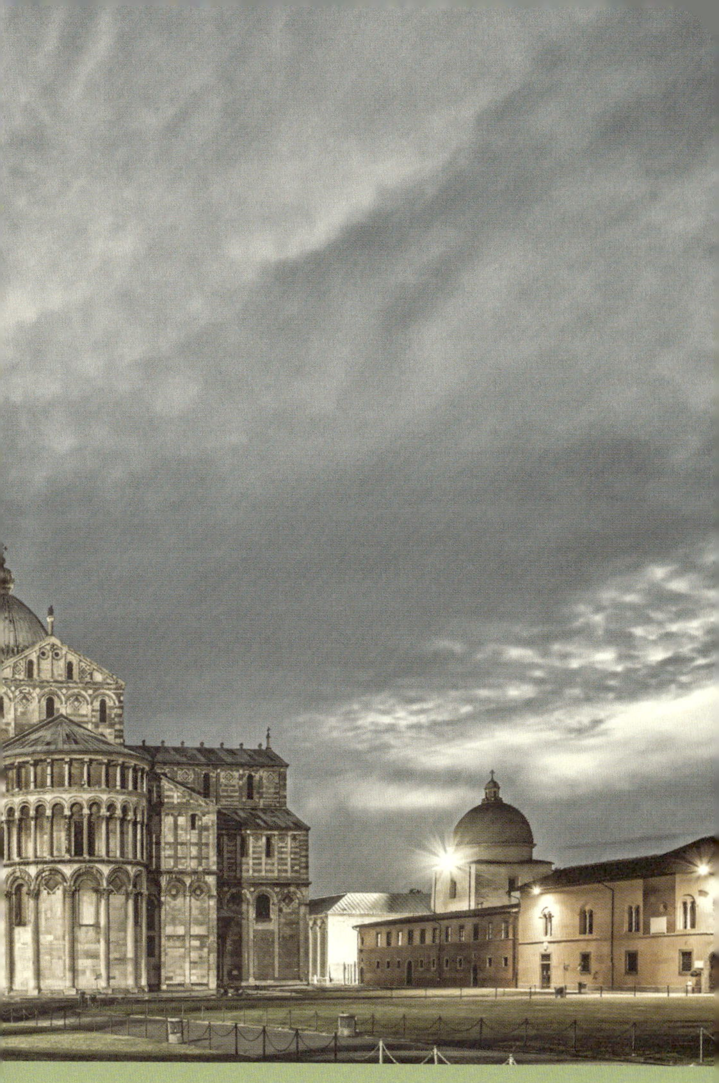

secoli è stata studiata, restaurata e "raddrizzata" più di una volta. Curioso che molti pisani non abbiano mai salito i 276 gradini necessari per arrivare in cima: secondo la tradizione porterebbe sfortuna a chi è nato e cresciuto a Pisa.

* See end pages for German and English translation

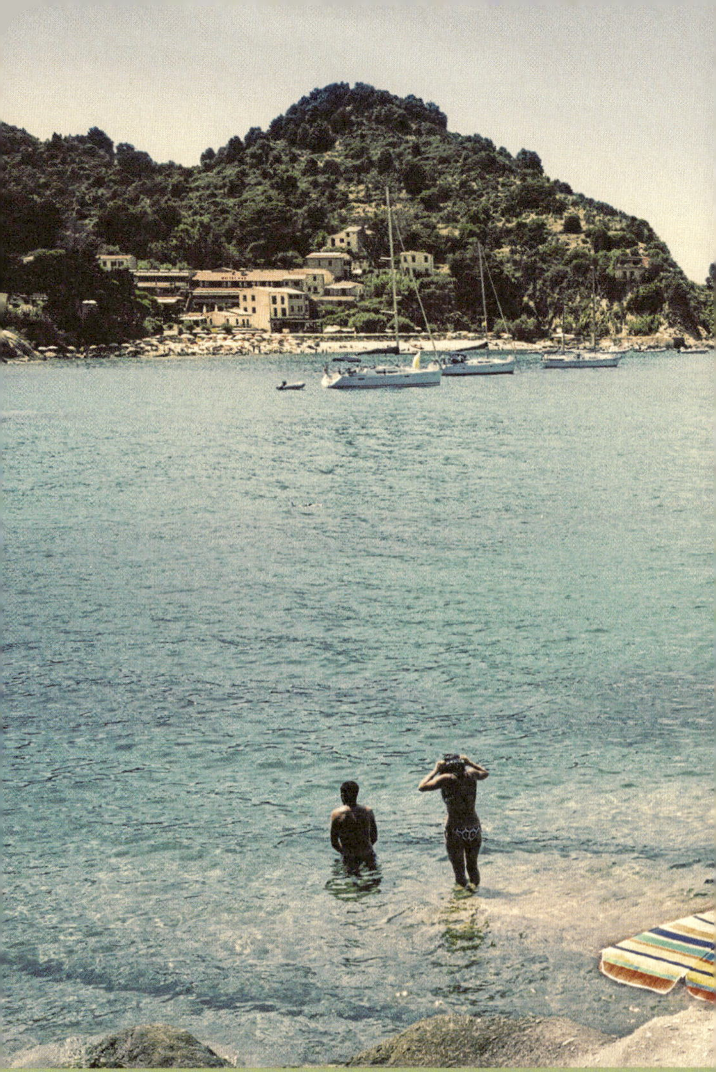

8

L'Isola d'Elba e Sant'Andrea

Da Capo Sant'Andrea lisce rocce granitiche chiamate dagli elbani "Cote Piane" degradano fino alla spiaggia, dove, incuranti delle acque cristalline, una volta attraccavano navi di ogni tipo per caricare non minerali di ferro, ma il vino prodotto sui terrazzamenti della zona.

* See end pages for German and English translation

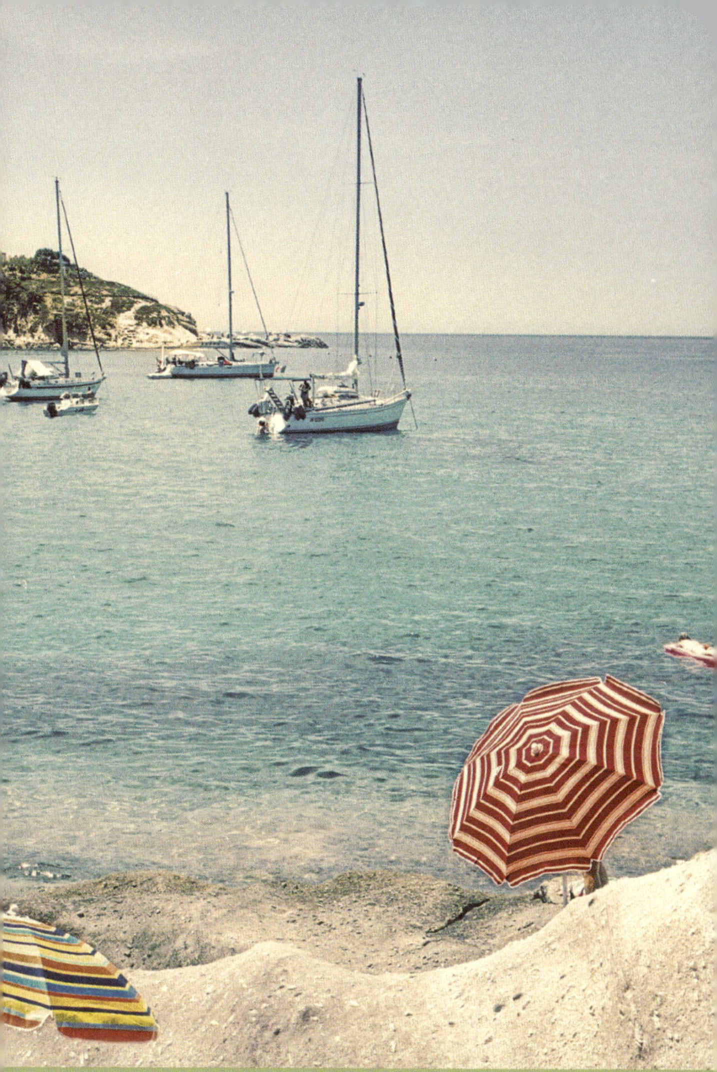

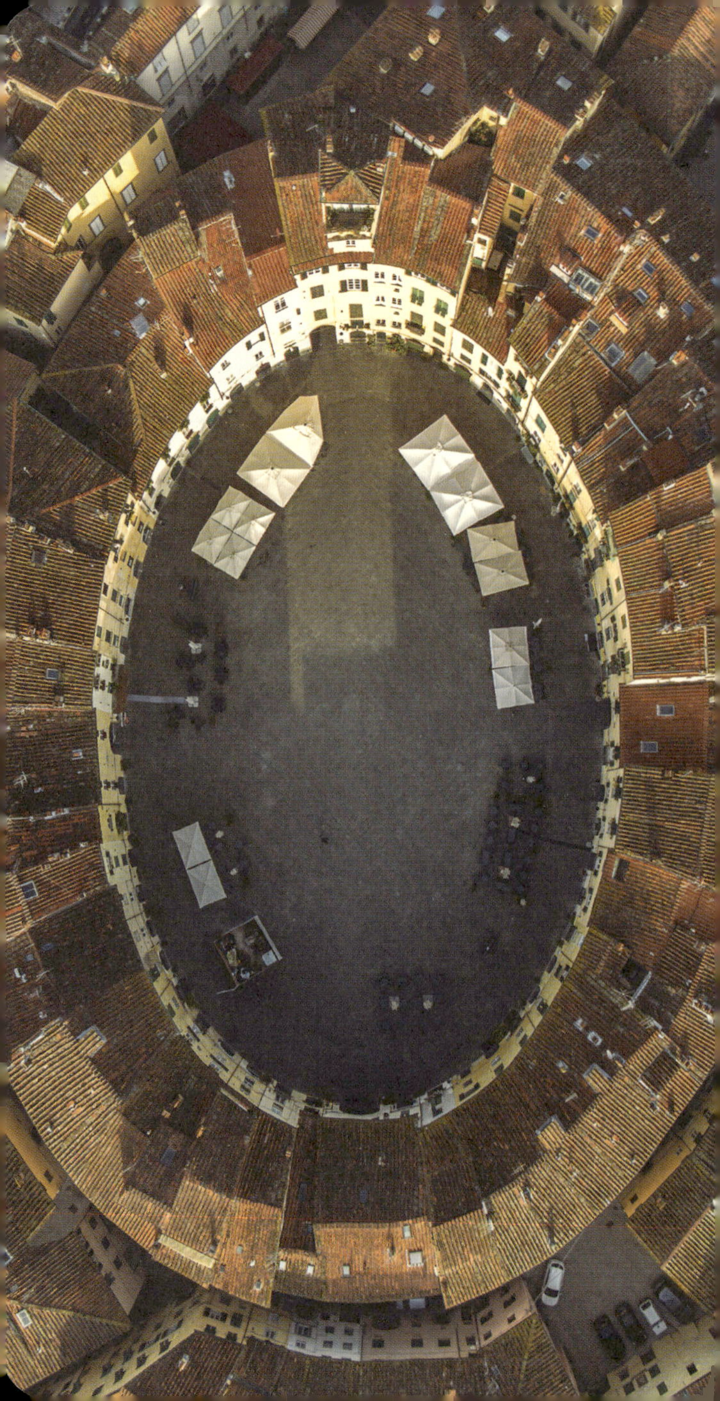

9

Piazza Anfiteatro

Costruito in Età Flavia con i sesterzi del cittadino Quinto Vibio, l'anfiteatro di Lucca aveva la classica forma ellittica e poteva contenere fino a 10000 spettatori. Usato come cava di materiale in epoca medievale, divenne in seguito deposito per il sale, polveriera e perfino carcere. Venne sistemato nell'Ottocento dall'architetto Lorenzo Nottolini che lasciò solo gli edifici che ne ricalcavano il perimetro esterno: nacque così una delle piazze più singolari d'Italia.

* See end pages for German and English translation

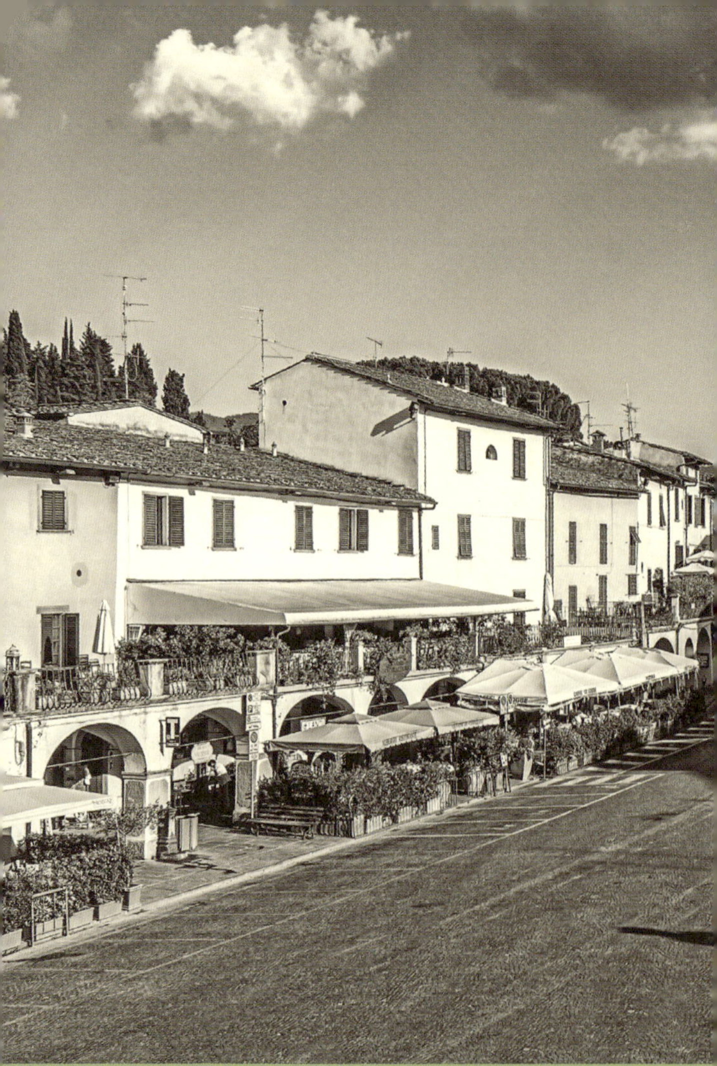

10

La Piazza di Greve in Chianti

In Toscana le zone in cui si tengono i mercati sono dette "mercatali". Fin dal XIII secolo abbiamo notizie certe del mercatale di Greve in Chianti. Trovandosi sulla direttrice Firenze-Siena era il più importante del Chianti. Oggi il mercato antico si svolge di sabato ed è ancora

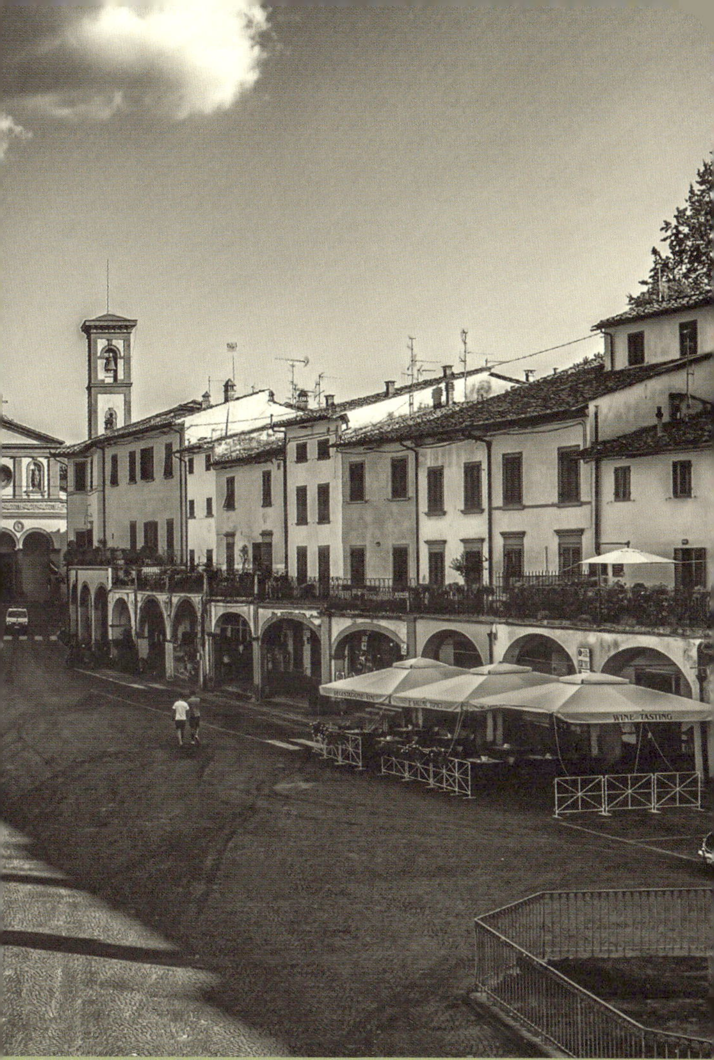

un'attrazione insieme alle botteghe, ai macellai, ai ristoranti situati sotto i portici di questa piazza a forma di imbuto.

* See end pages for German and English translation

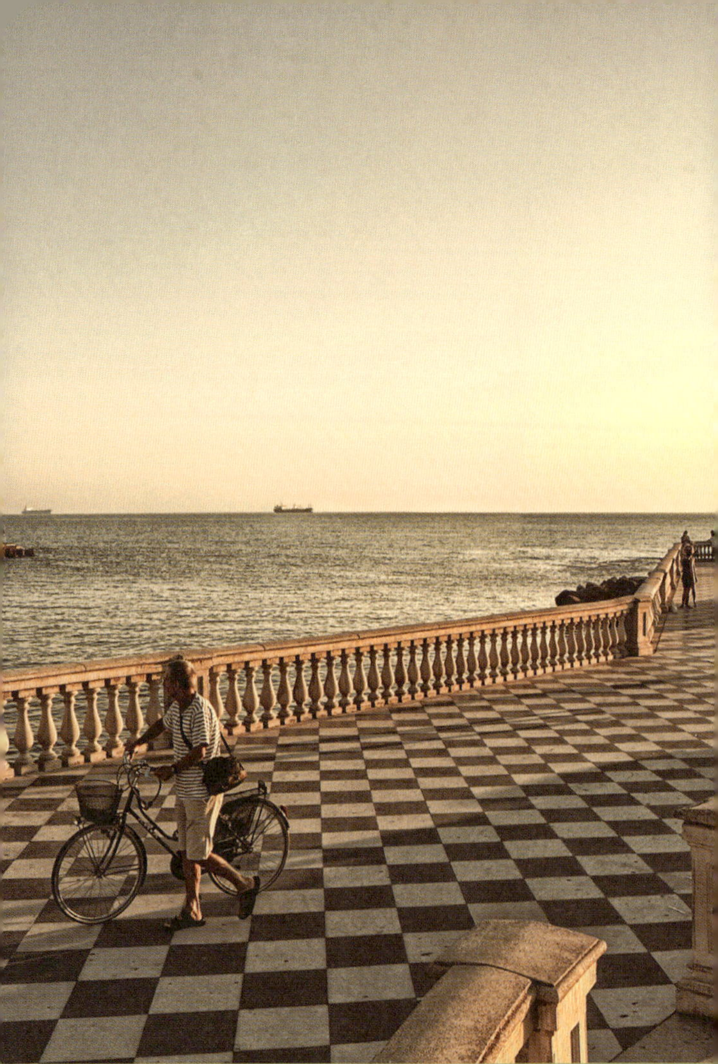

11

Terrazza Mascagni

In determinate ore del giorno potrebbe ricordare quasi un quadro surrealista di Salvador Dalì, con le sue 38000 piastrelle bianche e nere e le sue 4000 colonnine. La Terrazza Mascagni è il luogo più suggestivo di Livorno, un belvedere aperto sulle bellezze del mare.

* See end pages for German and English translation

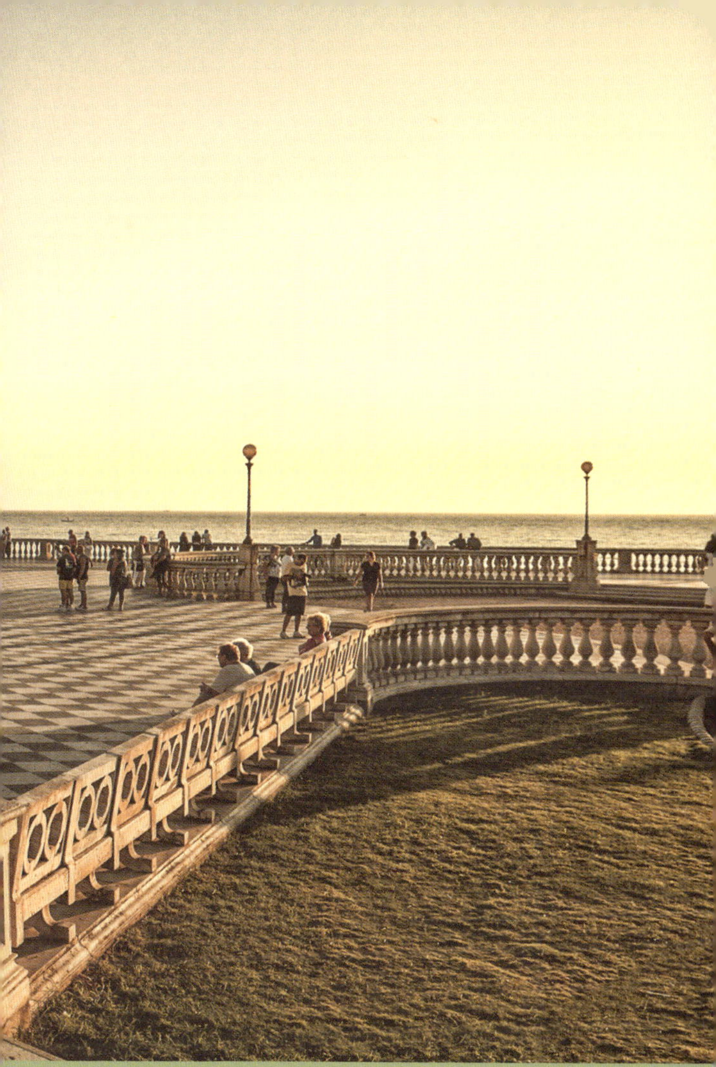

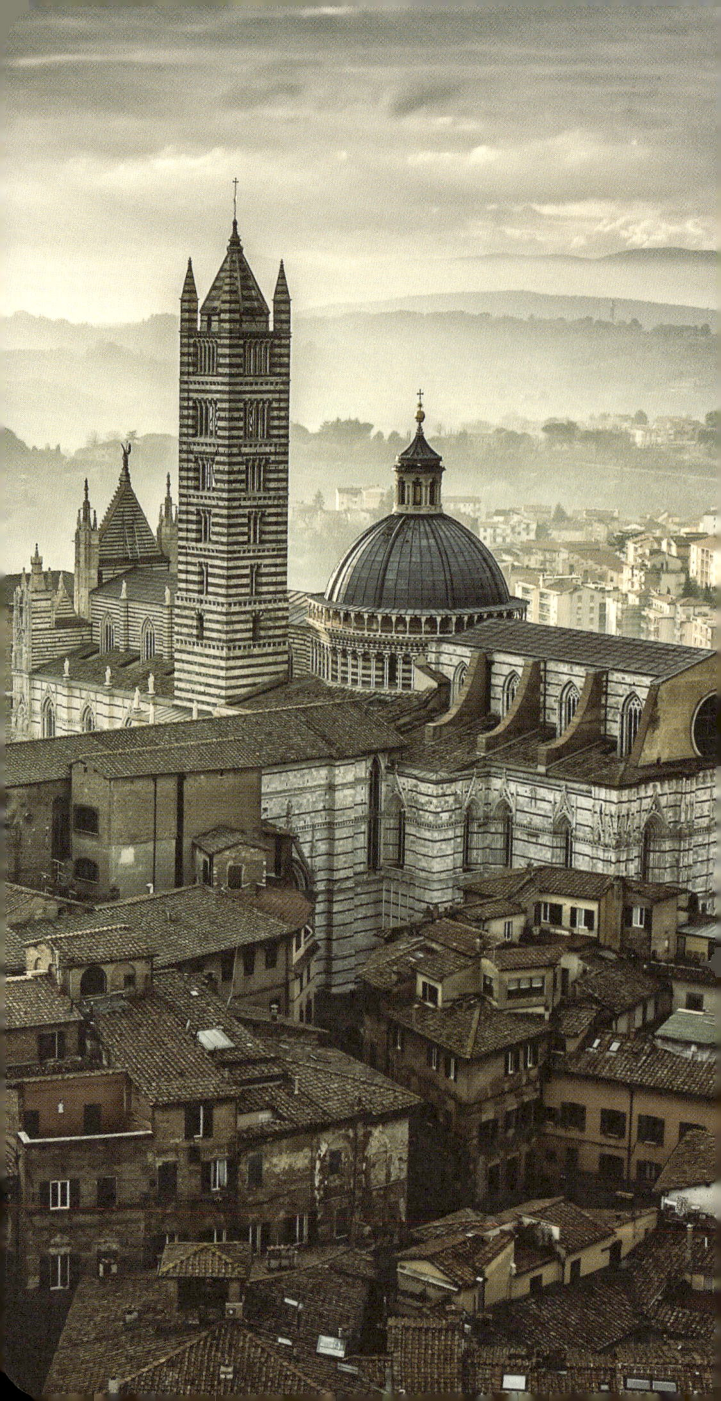

12

Duomo di Siena

La città era sempre più fiorente, il prestigio aumentava e nel Trecento a Siena si decise di costruire una nuova cattedrale che conferisse lustro alla città. Il progetto era imponente, l'attuale cattedrale ne avrebbe costituito solo il transetto. Purtroppo per problemi strutturali, ma soprattutto a causa della peste nera che colpì la città nel 1348, non venne mai portato a termine. In memoria ci rimane il "facciatone" che ci fa intuire la mole dell'edificio, quasi un fuori scala. Malgrado tutto la cattedrale fu poi ultimata in modo splendido ed è considerata uno dei migliori esempi di romanico gotico italiano.

* See end pages for German and English translation

13

Bagno Vignoni

Non si fatica molto ad immaginare Lorenzo il Magnifico o Papa Pio II in Piazza delle Sorgenti a Bagno Vignoni. All'epoca la stazione termale era molto frequentata: si trovava lungo la Via Francigena e vi sgorgavano acque solfuree a 49 gradi dai noti poteri benefici. Si narra che, però, Lapa, la madre della futura Santa Caterina da Siena, non ne rimase molto soddisfatta e forse fu un bene: portava qui la figlia nella speranza che la mondanità del luogo la distogliesse dal desiderio di farsi monaca...

* See end pages for German and English translation

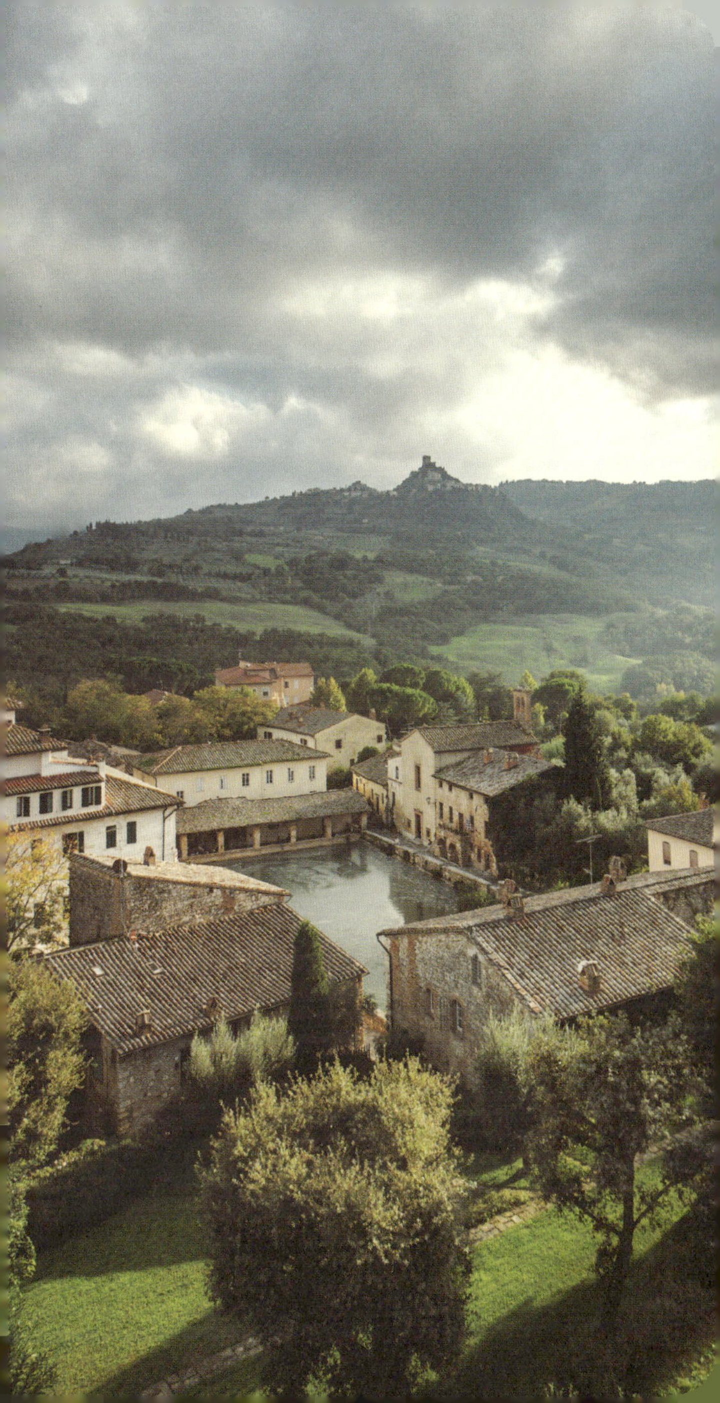

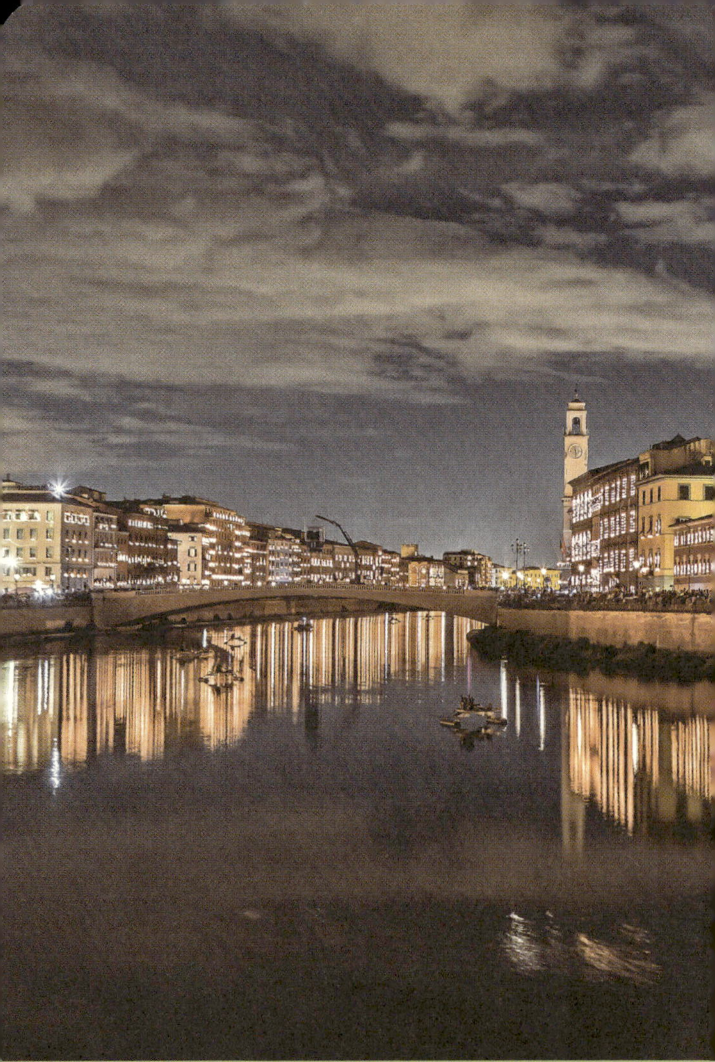

14

Luminara di San Ranieri

San Ranieri, fin dal Medioevo, fu molto venerato dal popolino del contado pisano come santo ladro, a causa della mancanza di un dito dello scheletro, dovuto – pare – ad un furto di formaggio prima del suo eremitaggio. Il corpo di Ranieri degli Scaccieri fu spostato in una nuova teca del Duomo di Pisa alla fine del XVII secolo, un luogo certamente più prestigioso per l'ormai patrono ufficiale della città. Per festeggiare

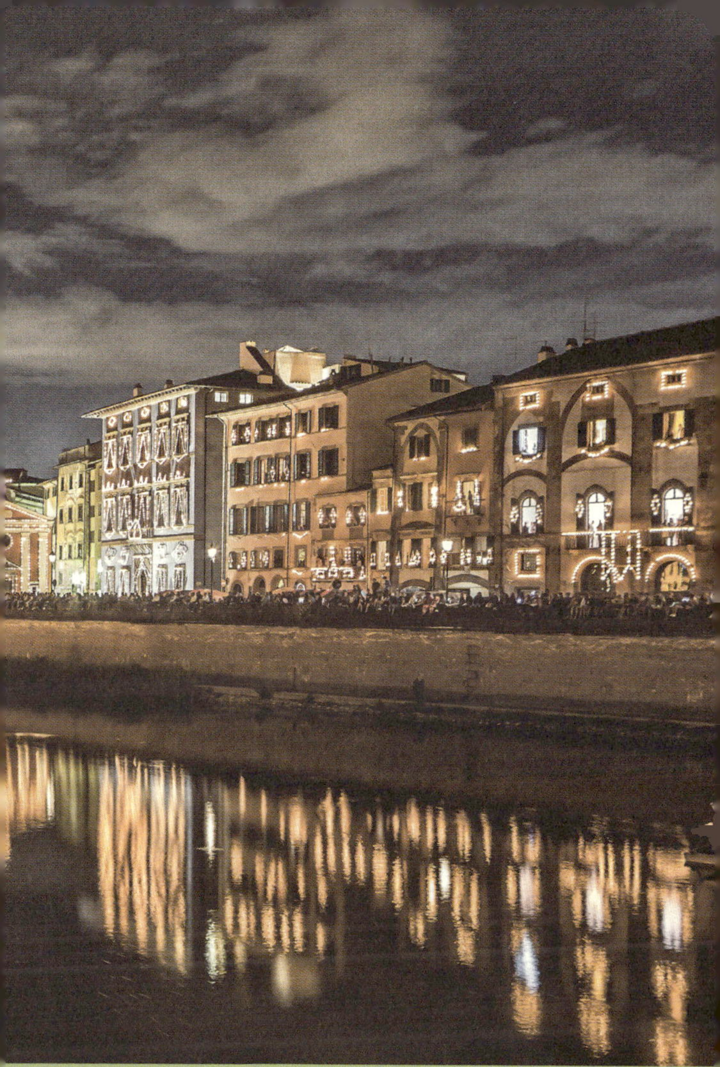

si illuminò la città con migliaia di candele. Inizialmente le strisce di luce delle candele disegnavano sul lungarno edifici fantastici. Oggigiorno, il 16 giugno di ogni anno, l'illuminazione segue i profili reali degli edifici con l'aggiunta di qualche paratura più fantasiosa e con spettacolo pirotecnico finale.

* See end pages for German and English translation

15

Palazzo Vecchio

Mirabile esempio di architettura civile trecentesca il Palazzo dei Priori, o Palazzo della Signoria, divenne "vecchio" quando nel 1550 Eleonora di Toledo acquistò Palazzo Pitti stabilendovi la residenza dei Medici. Singolare la maestosa Torre di Arnolfo, decentrata rispetto al corpo dell'edificio. Alta 94 metri, fu costruita su una torre preesistente detta "della Vacca" appartenente alla famiglia Foraboschi. La Torre poggia direttamente sul terreno e non sulla struttura del palazzo.

* See end pages for German and English translation

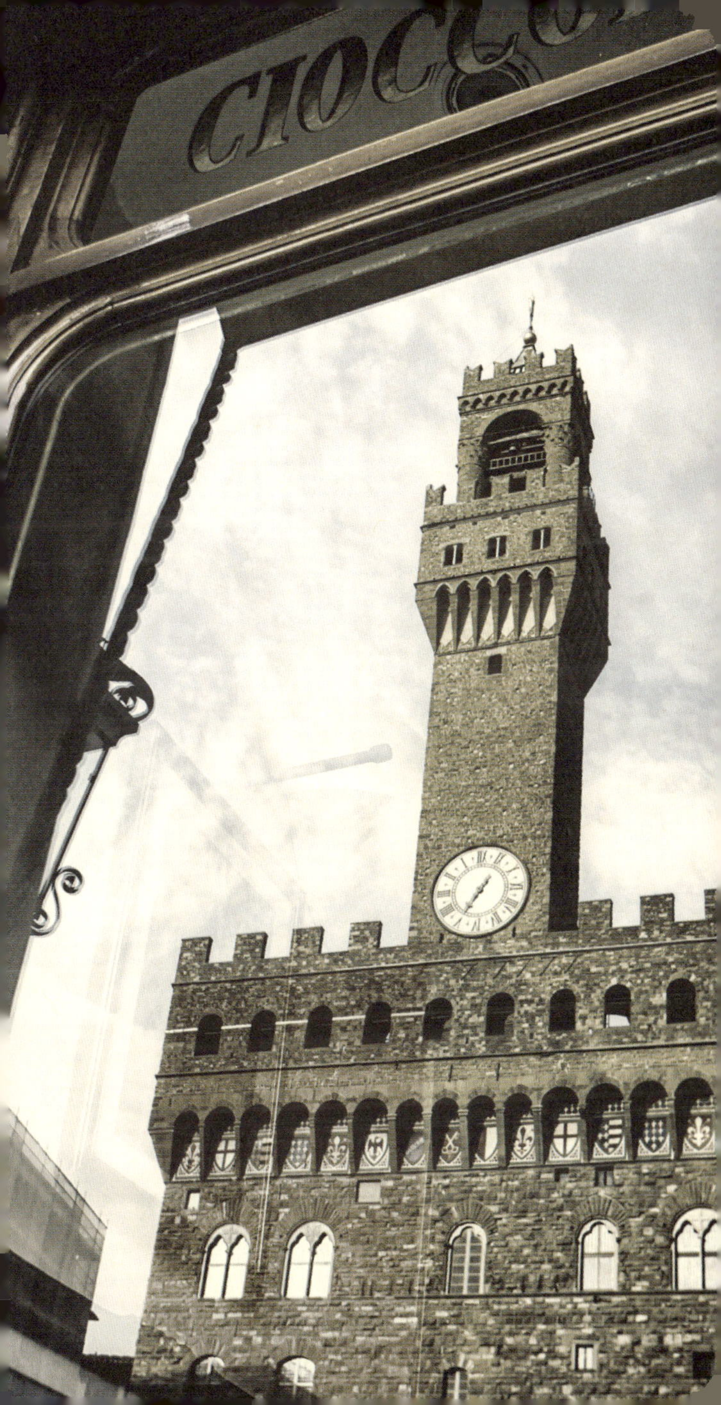

16

Giugno Pisano

Durante il Giugno Pisano si svolgono a Pisa una serie di manifestazioni in onore del patrono, San Ranieri. Spiccano per importanza il Gioco del Ponte, la Regata di San Ranieri e la Luminara di San Ranieri. L'ultimo sabato del mese, al tramonto, il Corteo Storico, con ben 709 figuranti, introduce il Gioco del Ponte, dove si affrontano i quartieri di Tramontana e Mezzogiorno in una prova di forza sul ponte di Mezzo.

* See end pages for German and English translation

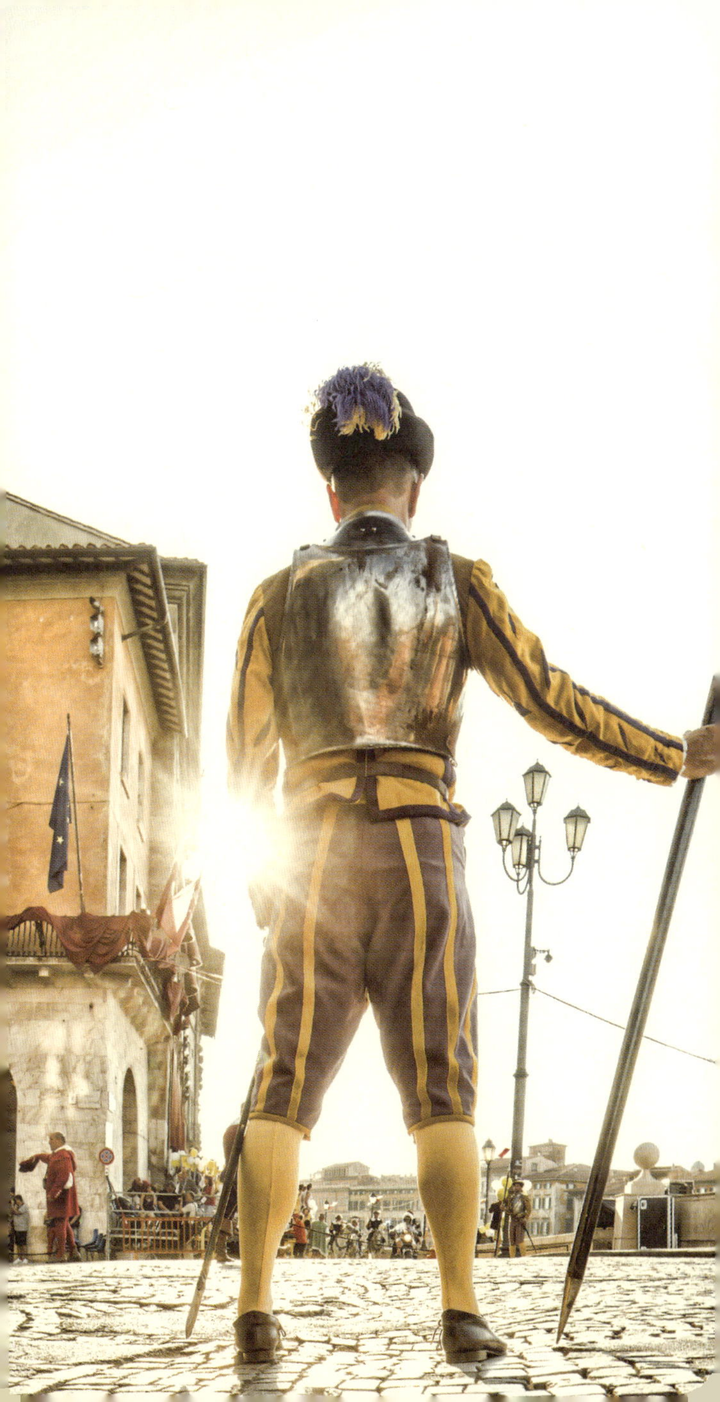

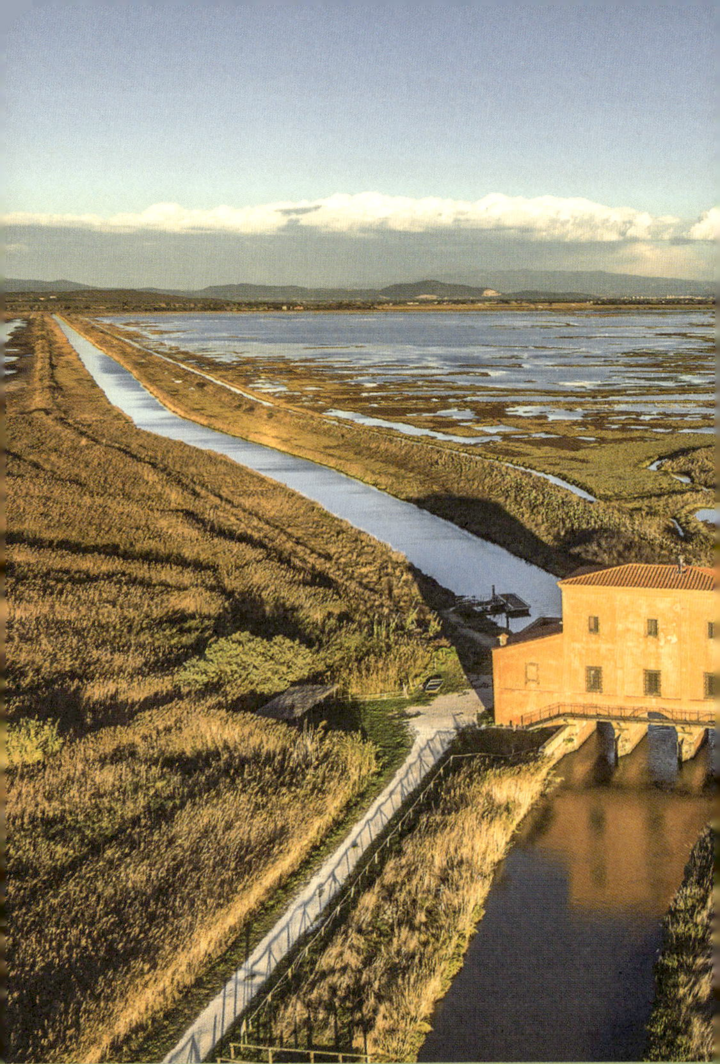

17

Casa Rossa Ximenes

La "fabbrica delle cataratte" fu costruita dal gesuita Leonardo Ximenes nel 1765 su incarico di Pietro Leopoldo di Lorena durante la bonifica della Maremma. L'edificio aveva il compito di tenere separate le acque del Padule di Castiglione e quelle del mare: si credeva infatti

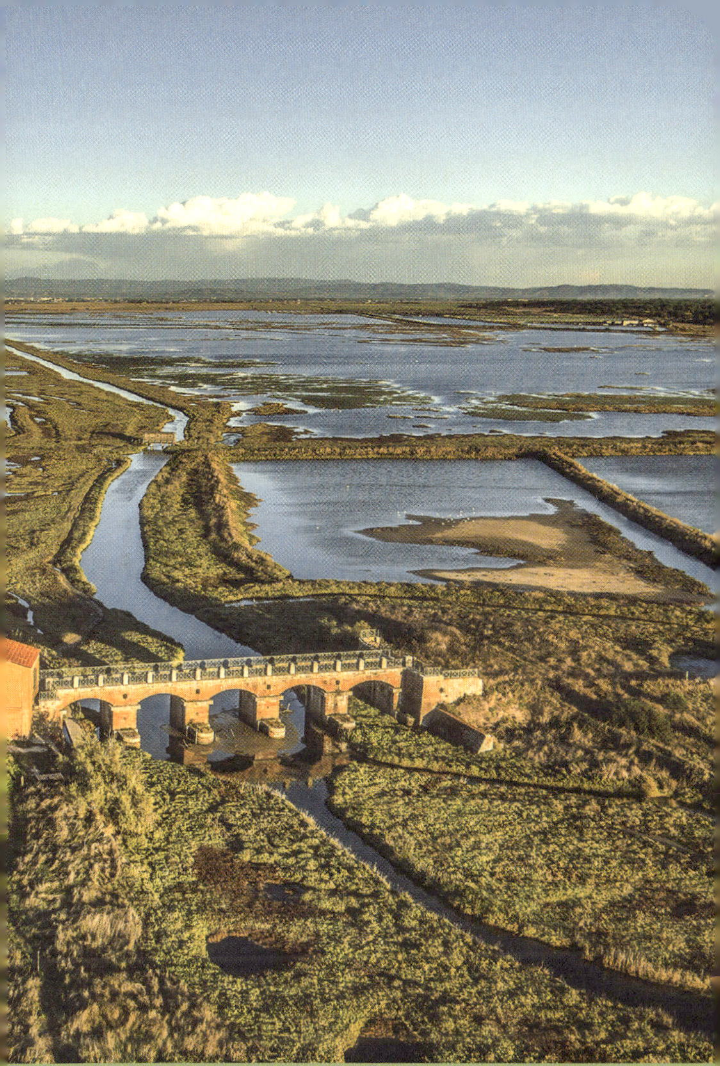

che la malaria avesse origine dal malsano mescolarsi delle acque dolci con quelle salmastre.

* See end pages for German and English translation

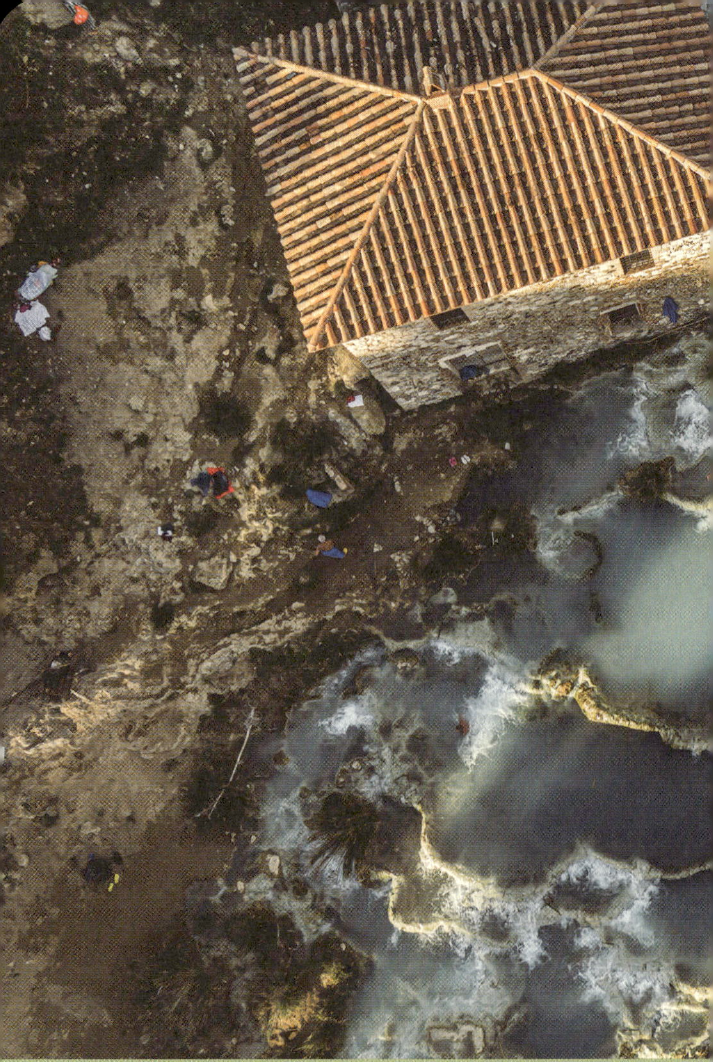

18

Cascate del Mulino a Saturnia

Secondo The Guardian e The New York Times, sono una delle destinazioni da vedere almeno una volta nella vita. I locali le chiamano Cascatelle e sono formate dalle acque solfuree del torrente Gorello. La loro temperatura è di 37 gradi e sono ricchissime di proprietà benefiche.

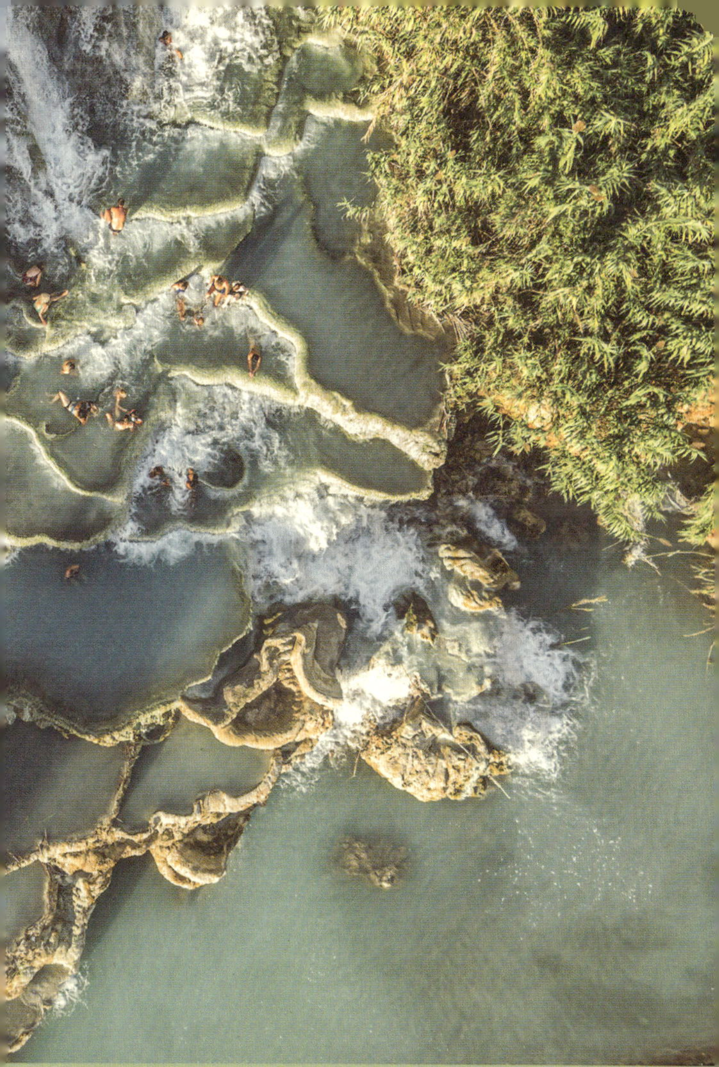

In inverno, con il freddo, densi vapori si alzano dalle acque rendendo il luogo molto suggestivo.

* See end pages for German and English translation

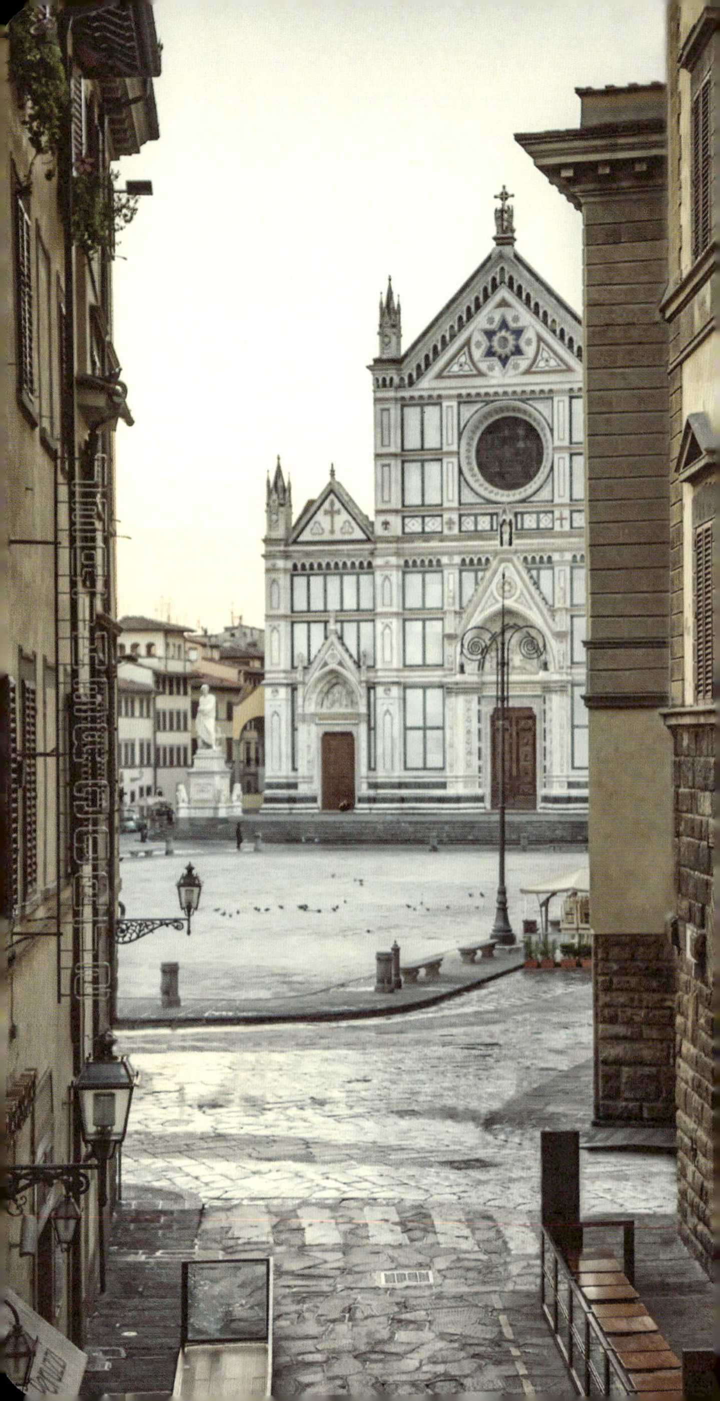

19

La Basilica di Santa Croce

"Ero già in una sorta di estasi all'idea di trovarmi a Firenze (...) Assorbito nella contemplazione della bellezza sublime, la vedevo da vicino, la toccavo per così dire. Ero giunto a quel livello di emozione, dove si incontrano le sensazioni celestiali date dalle arti e i sentimenti appassionati. Uscendo da Santa Croce, ebbi un tuffo al cuore, la vita per me si era inaridita, camminavo temendo di cadere" (Stendhal, Viaggio in Italia). In breve a Santa Croce nasce la celebre affezione psicosomatica conosciuta come Sindrome di Stendhal o di Firenze.

* See end pages for German and English translation

20

Piazza Grande ad Arezzo

Uno dei più illustri personaggi nati ad Arezzo è senza dubbio Giorgio Vasari. Nel 1573 per permettere al sommo artista la costruzione del Palazzo delle Logge, Piazza Grande venne completamente ristrutturata e ridotta alle dimensioni attuali. Nell'insieme le sobrie linee rinascimentali del Palazzo bene si combinano con le preesistenze medievali, conferendo all'insieme una certa eleganza. Addirittura, nel 1687, si proibisce alla "plebaglia" di passeggiare sotto il loggiato per mantenerne il decoro...

* See end pages for German and English translation

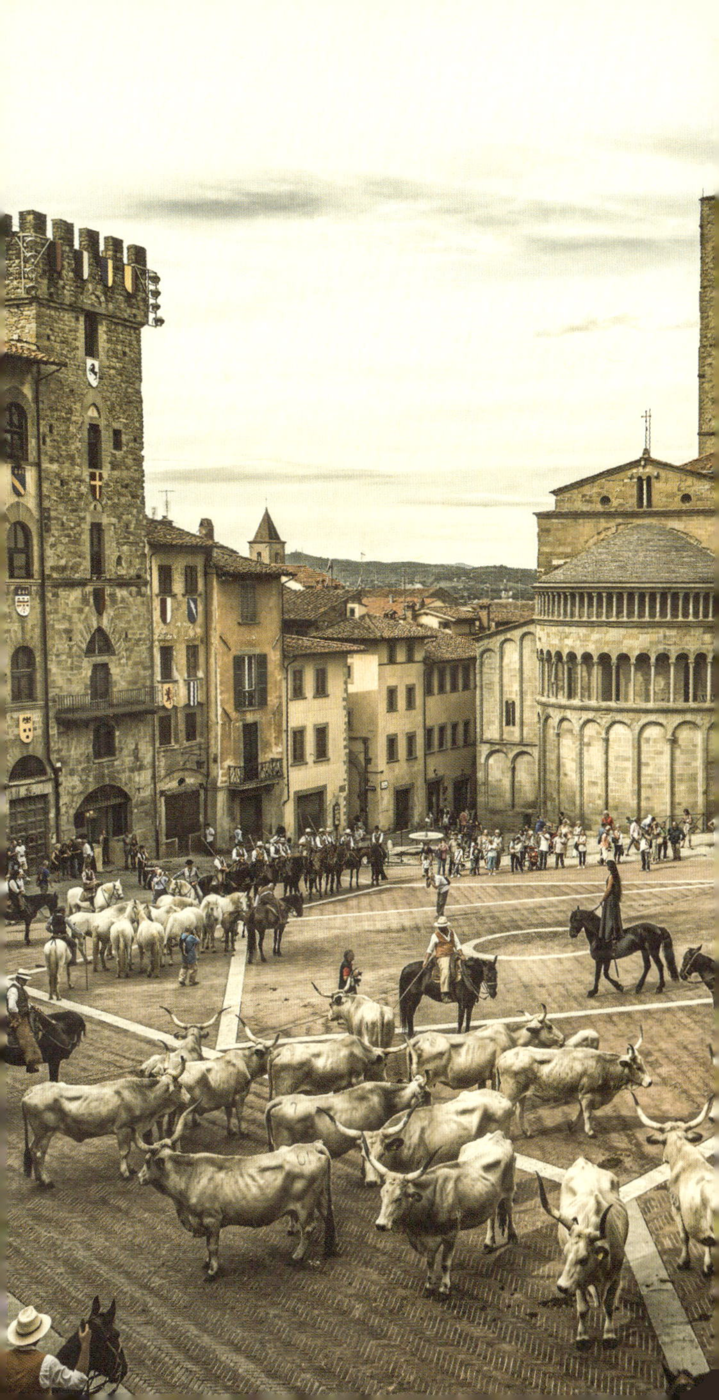

21

Brunello di Montalcino

Il Brunello di Montalcino nasce nel 1865. La crescita del vino in questo secolo e mezzo abbondante è stata esponenziale ed è ormai diventato a livello qualitativo un riferimento internazionale. Il pioniere del Brunello fu Clemente Santi, seguito dal nipote Ferruccio Biondi, che selezionò il Sangiovese Grosso come vitigno adatto alla lunga stagionatura anche in purezza. Nel 1888 venne imbottigliata la prima bottiglia di Brunello Riserva. L'ultima volta che ne è stata aperta una è stato nel 1994 in occasione della Degustazione del Centenario.

* See end pages for German and English translation

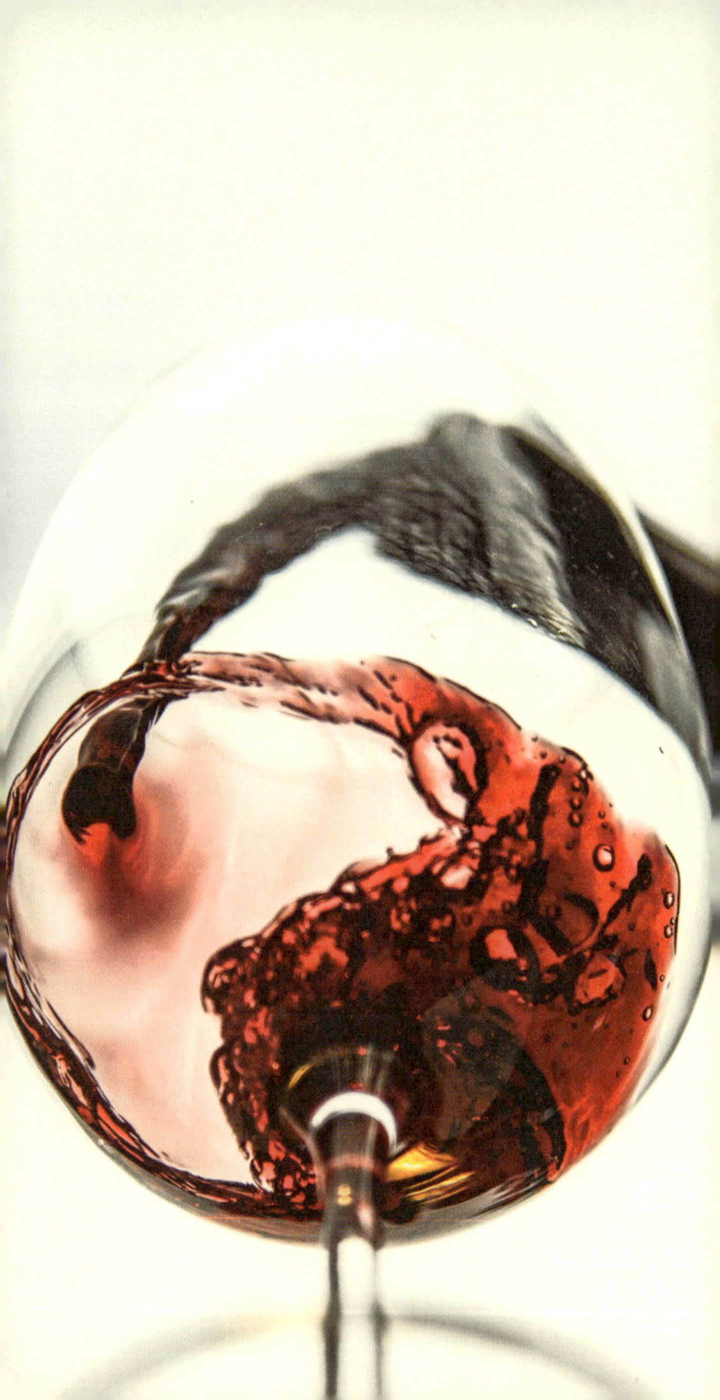

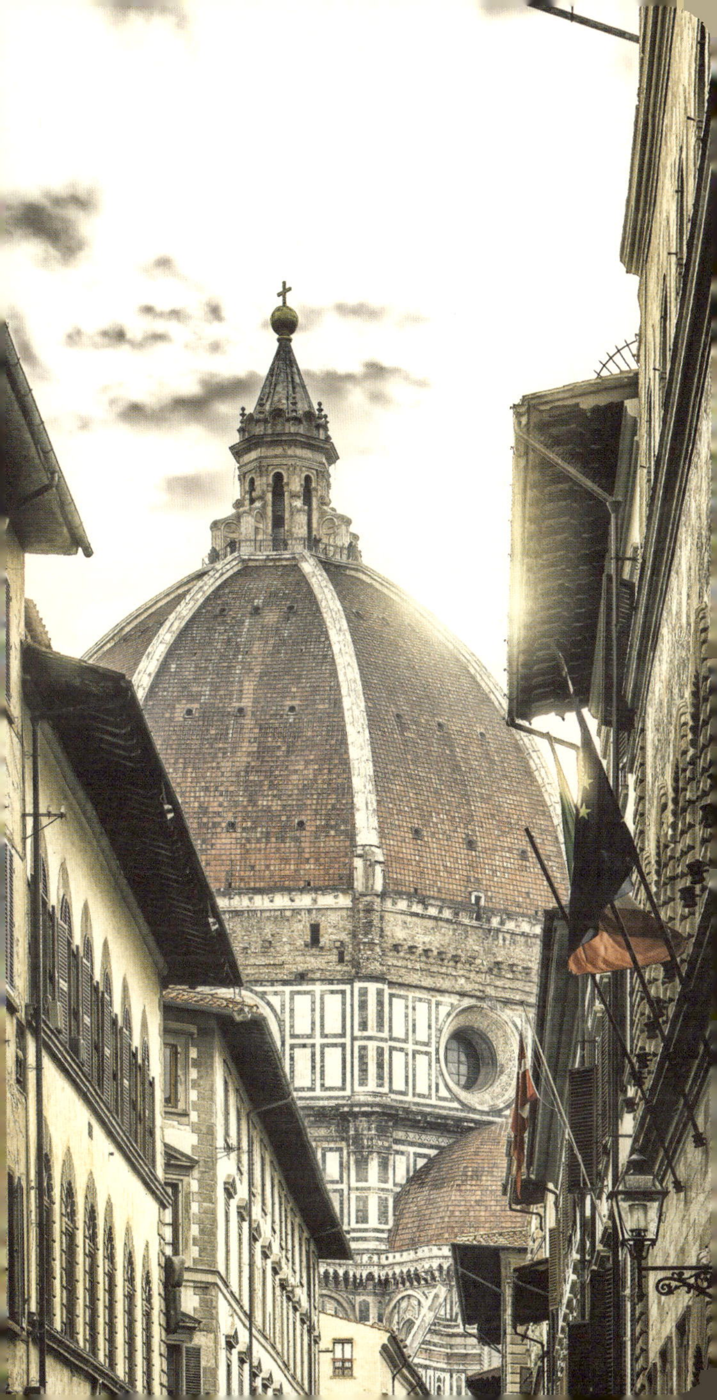

22

Via dei Servi

È da Via dei Servi, guardando in alto verso i tetti irregolari, che ci si rende conto della maestosità della Cupola. Così grande che, secondo il Vasari, durante la costruzione c'erano delle taverne installate sui ponteggi per evitare i tempi morti che avrebbe richiesto lo scendere e il salire dei lavoratori per mangiare.

* See end pages for German and English translation

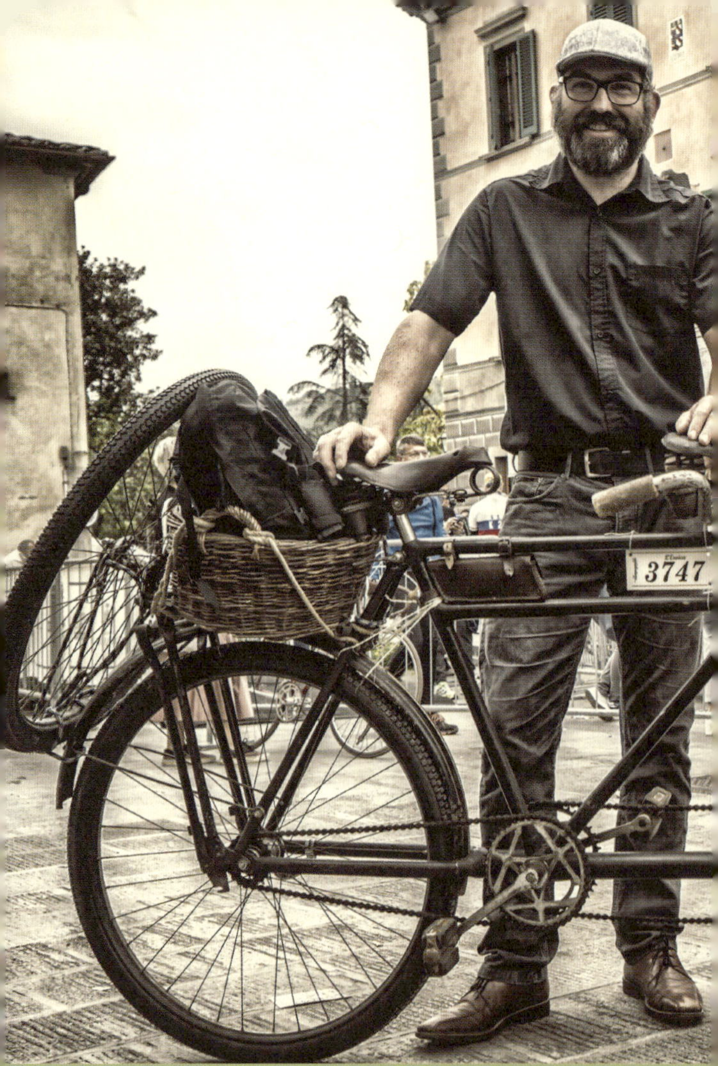

23

L'Eroica

Poteva sembrare semplicemente nostalgia: nostalgia di un ciclismo fatto di sudore, di fango, di strade sterrate, insomma di un ciclismo ormai andato. Invece l'idea di Giancarlo Brocci di creare una manifestazione di nicchia, per pochi eletti, basata su valori che sembravano tramontati, si è rivelata un successo planetario, creando

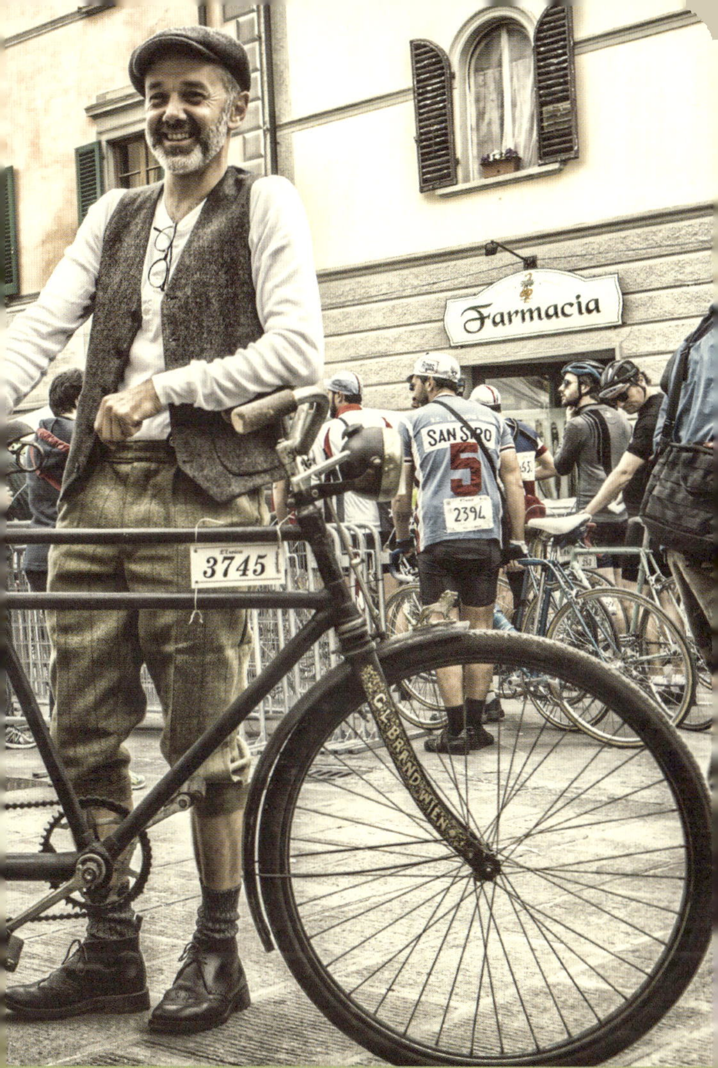

addirittura moda e tendenza. La consacrazione? Nel 2010 si corre una tappa del Giro d'Italia proprio sul percorso dell'Eroica, si arriva a Montalcino. Una tappa terribile, tutta sotto la pioggia, al traguardo arrivano maschere di fango stremate: il ciclismo come evocazione della fatica si è ritrovato...

* See end pages for German and English translation

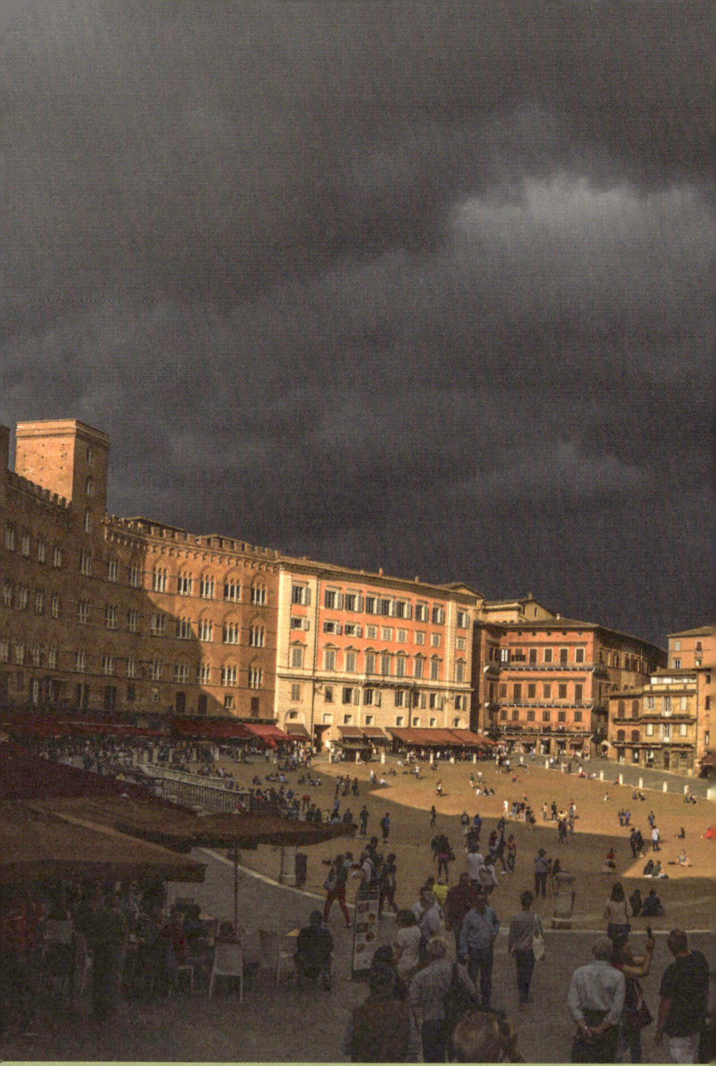

24

Piazza del Campo

Piazza dalla forma singolare, "a conchiglia" appunto, è pavimentata in cotto a coda di pesce suddiviso in nove spicchi da direttrici in travertino bianco. Gli spicchi rappresentano praticamente i governatori del "Governo dei Nove" e, metaforicamente, le pieghe del Mantello della

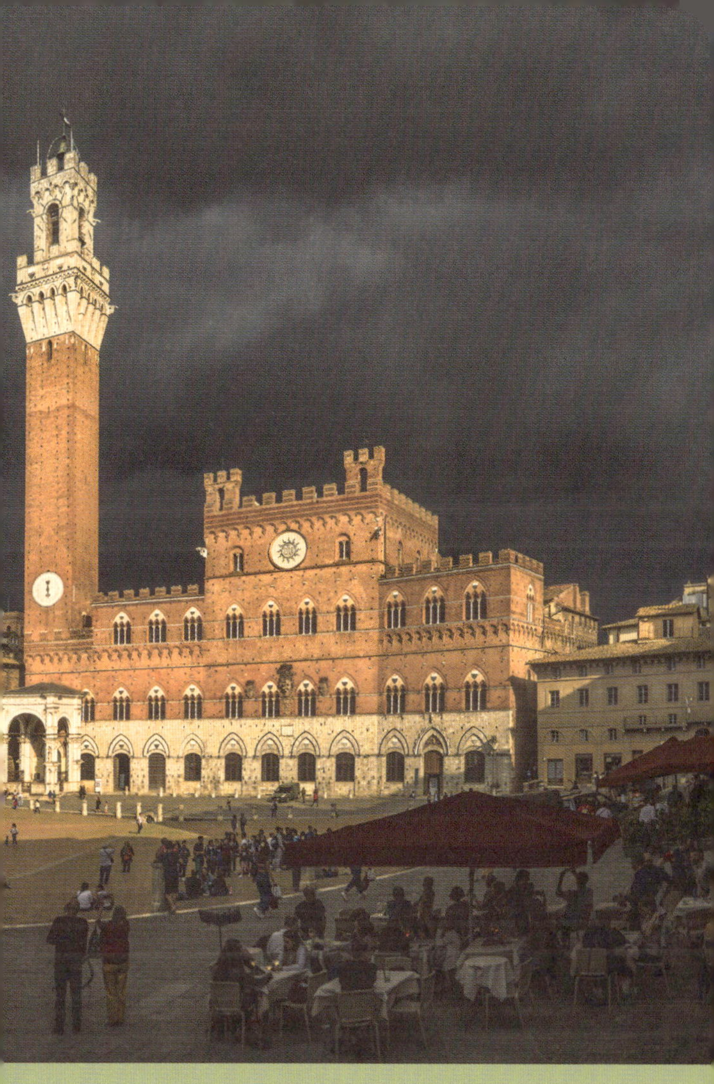

Vergine Maria. A Siena Piazza del Campo e il Palazzo Pubblico sono considerati terreno neutro... Secondo un'antica convenzione non fanno parte di nessuna delle 17 contrade in cui è divisa la città. Vi si corre il palio ed è giusto che sia così.

* See end pages for German and English translation

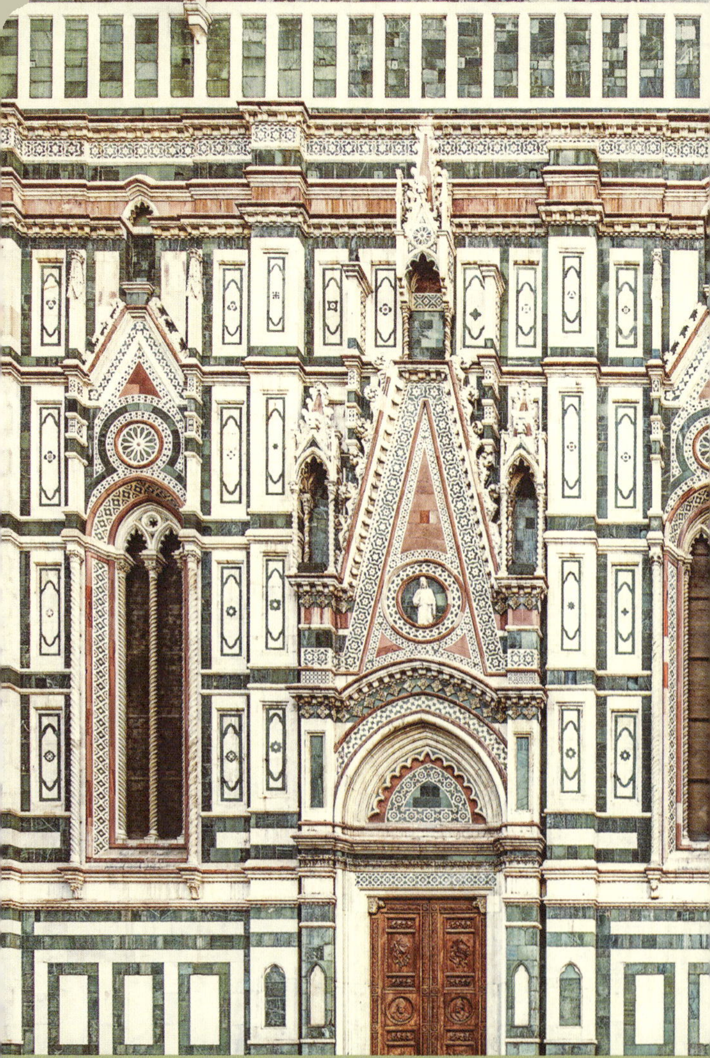

25

Santa Maria del Fiore

Per capire la Cattedrale di Santa Maria del Fiore a Firenze bisogna assolutamente visitare il nuovo Museo dell'Opera del Duomo. La storia è complessa, si passa dal progetto gotico di Arnolfo di Cambio, alla costruzione del Campanile di Giotto e della Cupola, fino ad arrivare

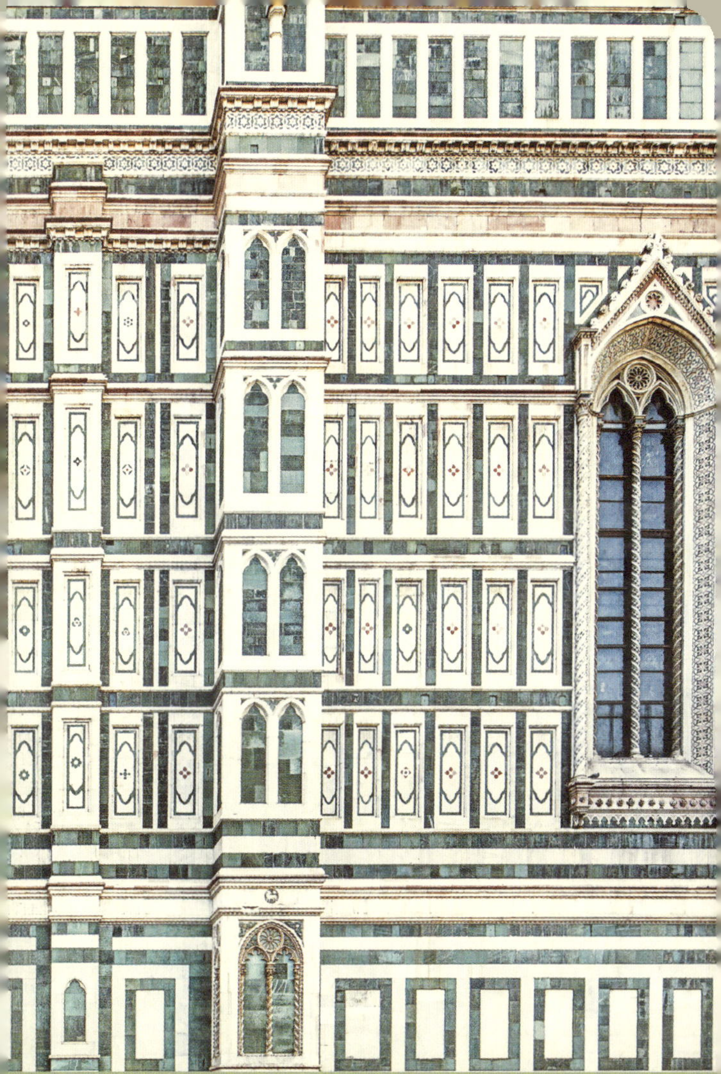

a quella che per Firenze è stata una vera e propria saga: "la facciata". Il Duomo aveva una facciata incompiuta in pietraforte, parzialmente dipinta. Dopo le usuali polemiche feroci, Firenze scelse il progetto di Emilio De Fabris in stile neogotico. La facciata fu inaugurata nel 1887.

* See end pages for German and English translation

26

Il David di Michelangelo

"- C'era una volta...
- Un re! - diranno subito i miei piccoli lettori.
- No, ragazzi, avete sbagliato. C'era una volta un pezzo di legno..."
(Collodi, Le Avventure di Pinocchio, 1881-1883)

Questa volta no, nel nostro caso si potrebbe dire "C'era una volta un pezzo di marmo...". Era un enorme pezzo di marmo di pessima qualità, pieno di venature e taroli (piccoli fori di pochi millimetri) che da tempo si trovava – quasi abbandonato – nei cantieri dell'Opera del Duomo; secondo la committenza da esso doveva nascere una statua di Re David da porre sui contrafforti del Duomo di Firenze. Eminenti artisti – Agostino di Duccio nel 1463-1464 e Antonio Rossellino nel 1476 – avevano rinunciato a realizzare l'opera e ormai il marmo era considerato *male abbozatum et sculptum*.

Michelangelo ricevette la commessa il 16 agosto 1501 per la somma di 400 fiorini. Dopo circa tre anni nacque il David e l'8 settembre 1504 venne presentato alla città: l'impressione che suscitò fu enorme.

* See end pages for German and English translation

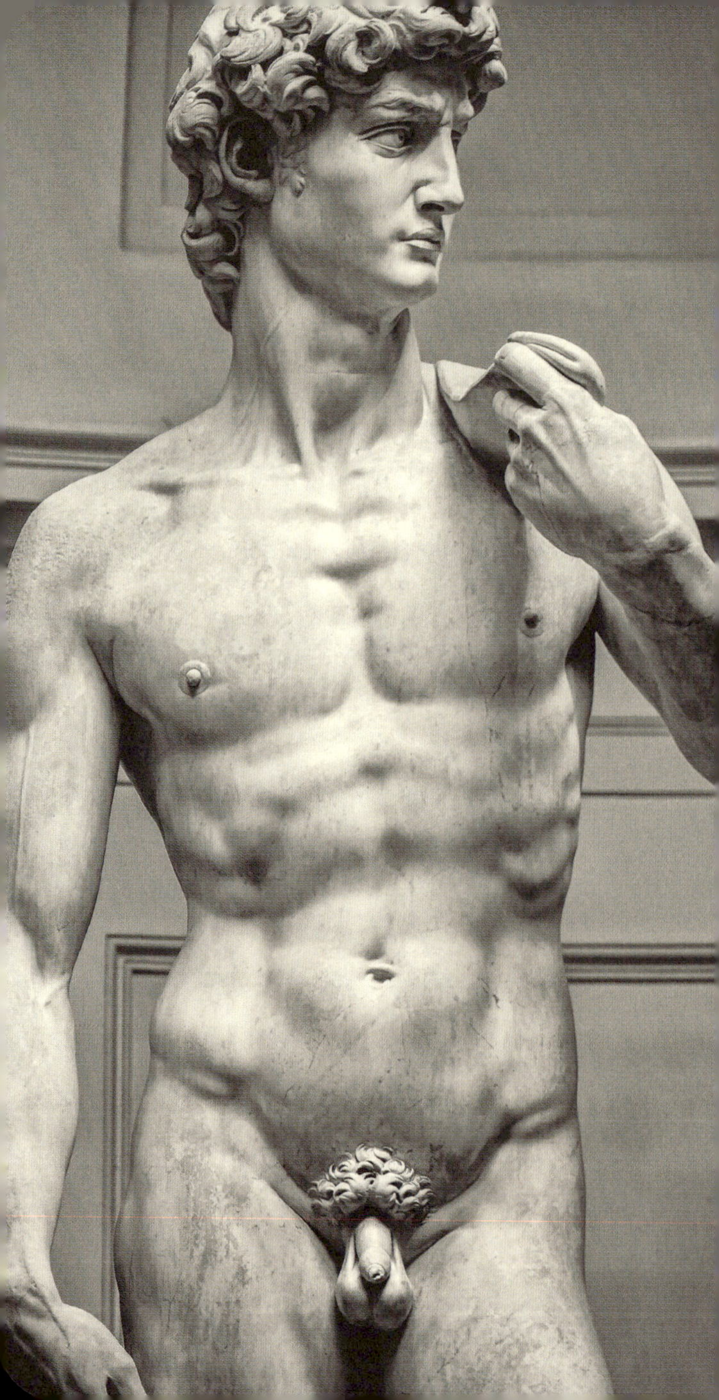

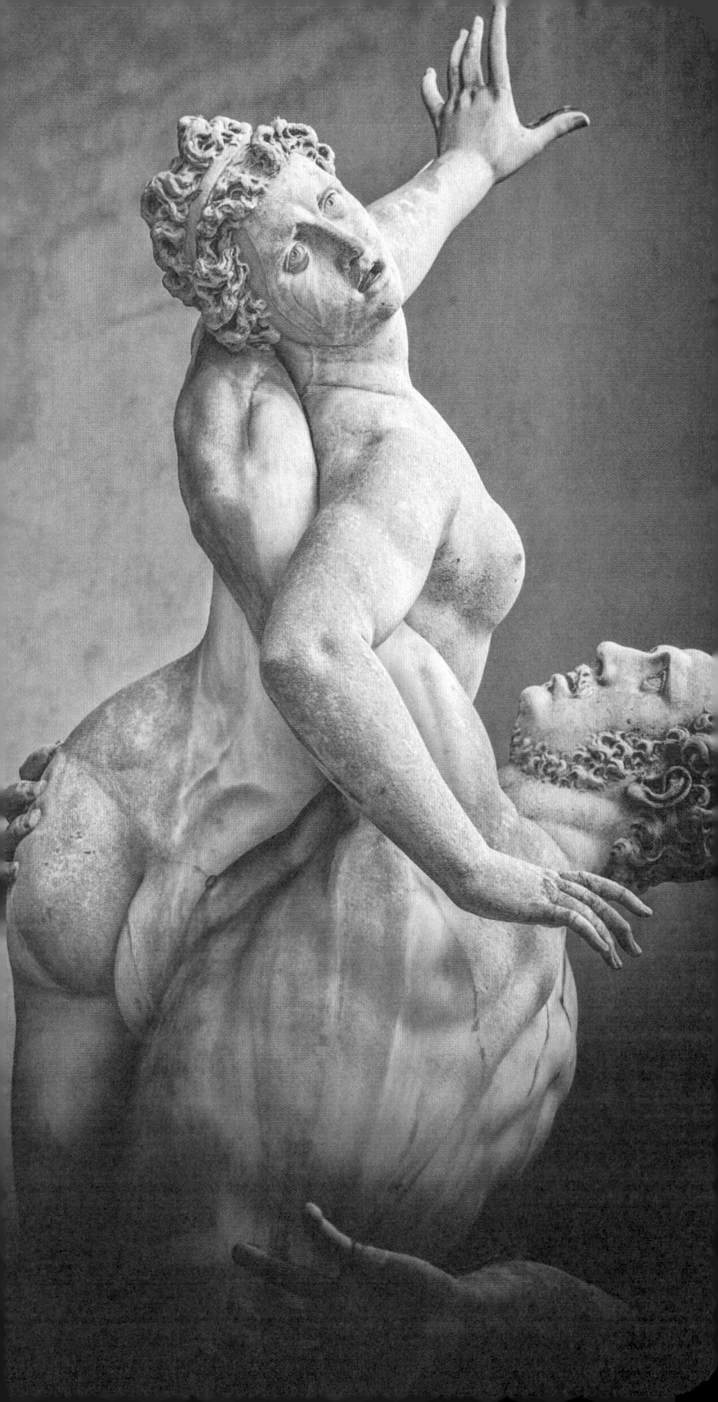

27

Il Ratto delle Sabine

Tre figure in marmo, un vecchio, un giovane e una fanciulla: siamo sotto la Loggia dei Lanzi a Firenze in Piazza della Signoria, un vero e proprio museo a cielo aperto. Ci si accorge subito che, per ammirare la scultura, non esiste un punto di vista privilegiato, ma girandoci intorno, allontanandosi e avvicinandosi, se ne scoprono nuovi particolari, nuovi intrecci, nuove prospettive...

Solo successivamente ribattezzata Ratto delle Sabine, è probabilmente il capolavoro della scultura manierista ed è opera del fiammingo Jean de Boulogne, comunemente conosciuto a Firenze come Giambologna.

* See end pages for German and English translation

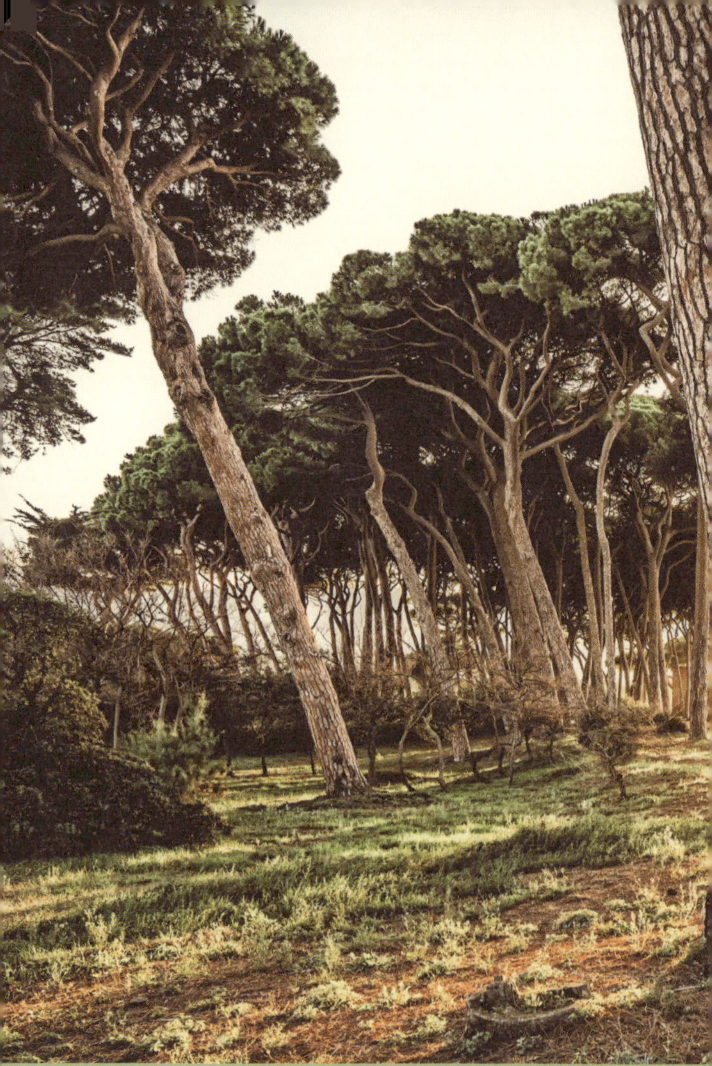

28

Baratti

Non è facile parlare di un luogo magico. Le sensazioni che provoca sono sottili, soggettive, chiuse dentro di te. Il Golfo di Baratti, con la spiaggia e la pineta, è sicuramente un luogo meraviglioso che emana un'aura particolare. Il luogo ha tempi propri anche d'estate, si spopola

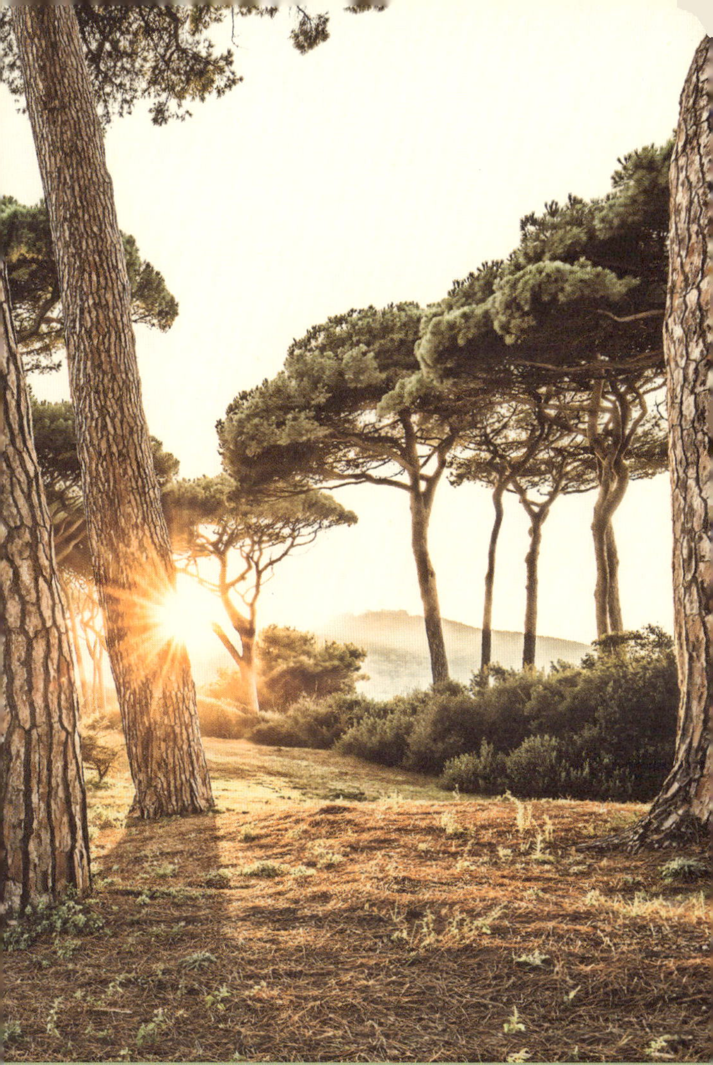

quasi inspiegabilmente all'imbrunire offrendo atmosfere bellissime. Altrettanto succede fuori stagione. La zona è praticamente deserta e la salita alla Rocca di Populonia ti arricchisce con gli odori della macchia mediterranea e scorci mozzafiato.

* See end pages for German and English translation

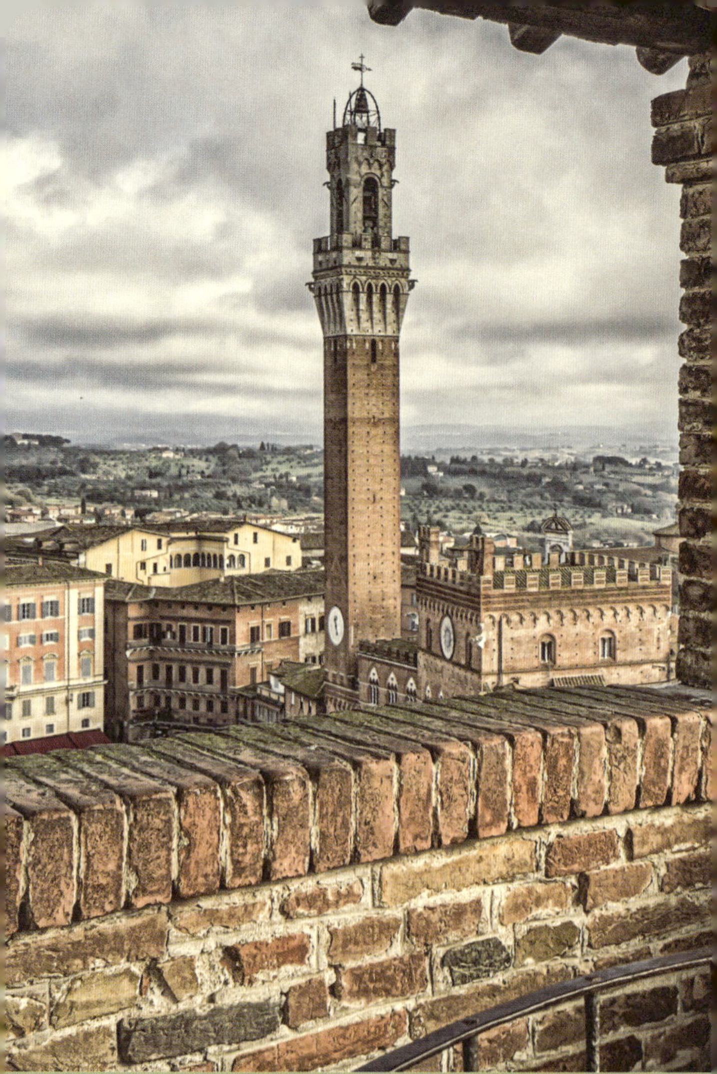

29

La Torre del Mangia

"Il Mangia" doveva essere famoso nelle osterie senesi del suo tempo. Vi spendeva tutto quello che guadagnava. Giovanni di Duccio – questo il suo vero nome – fu il primo campanaro e custode della torre del Palazzo Pubblico di Siena poco dopo il 1348. Dal suo soprannome deriva il nome della torre. Il suo lavoro durò poco, però. Nel 1360 venne installato il

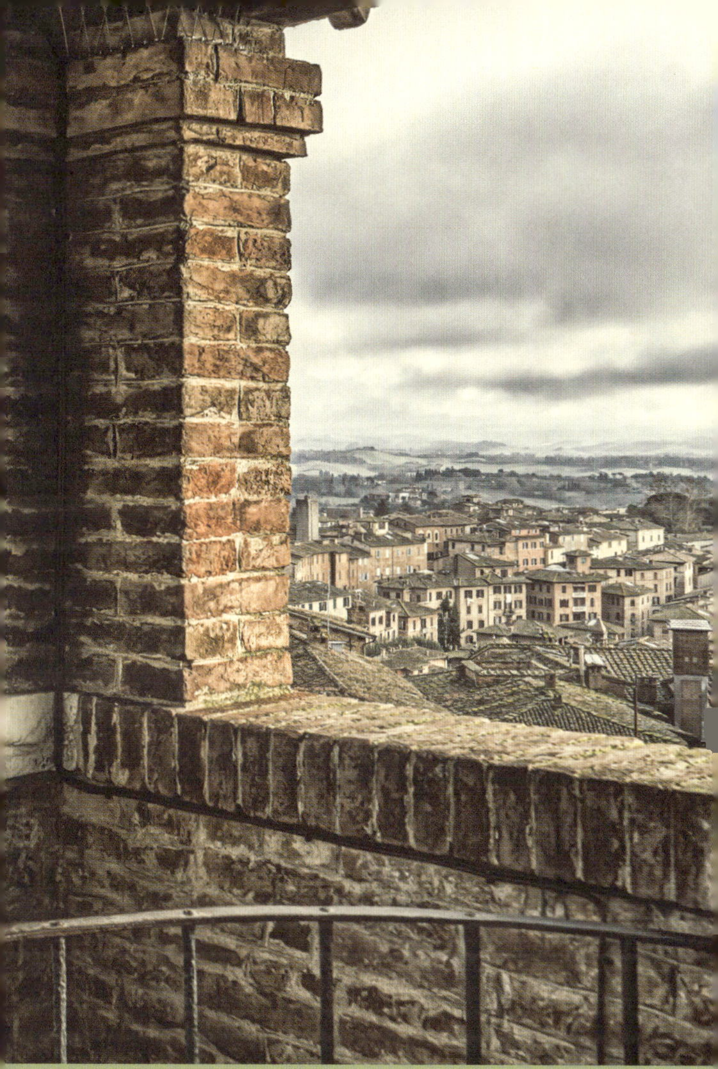

primo orologio meccanico con un automa che batteva le ore... e questo fu allo stesso tempo un errore, vista la travagliata storia della campana della torre, ed una rivincita per il "Mangia". Infatti la campana, battuta tuttora da un automa, suona sempre "sorda". Solo un giorno all'anno – il giorno del Palio – viene suonata manualmente e il suono è perfetto...

* See end pages for German and English translation

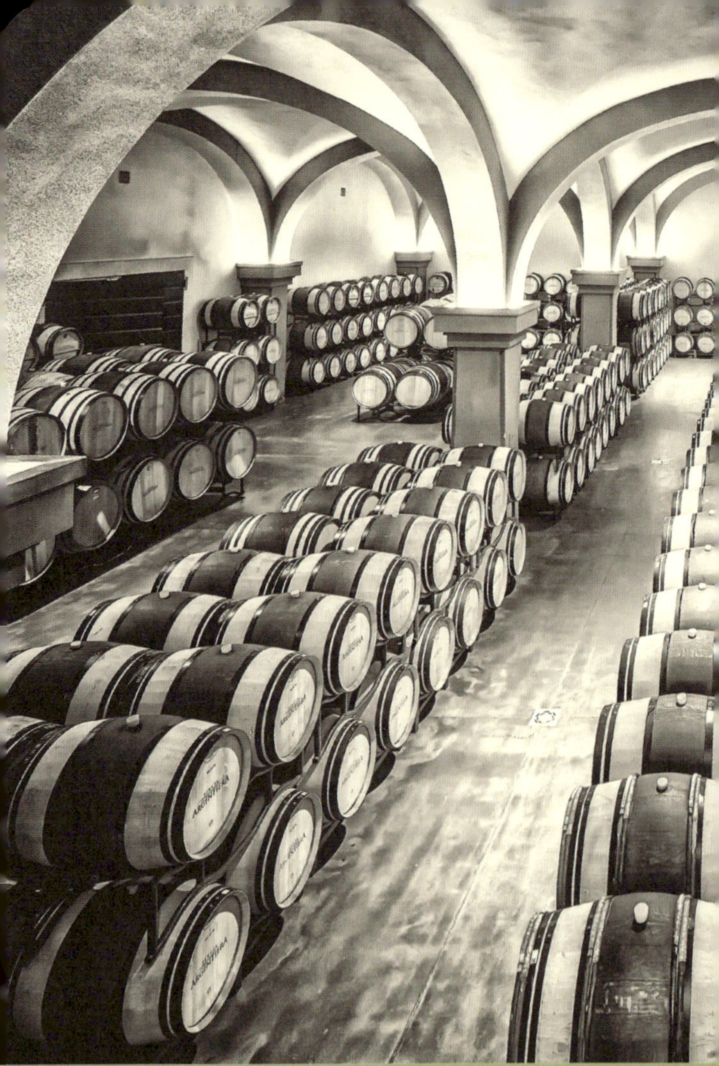

30

La Cantina della Tenuta Argentiera a Bolgheri

L'intuizione del marchese Incisa della Rocchetta si è rivelata vincente. Trasferitosi a Bolgheri dopo il matrimonio, fu lui che, ispirandosi agli amati vini francesi, provò ad impiantare una varietà di Cabernet presente a Migliarino, nei dintorni di Pisa. La vicinanza del mare fece

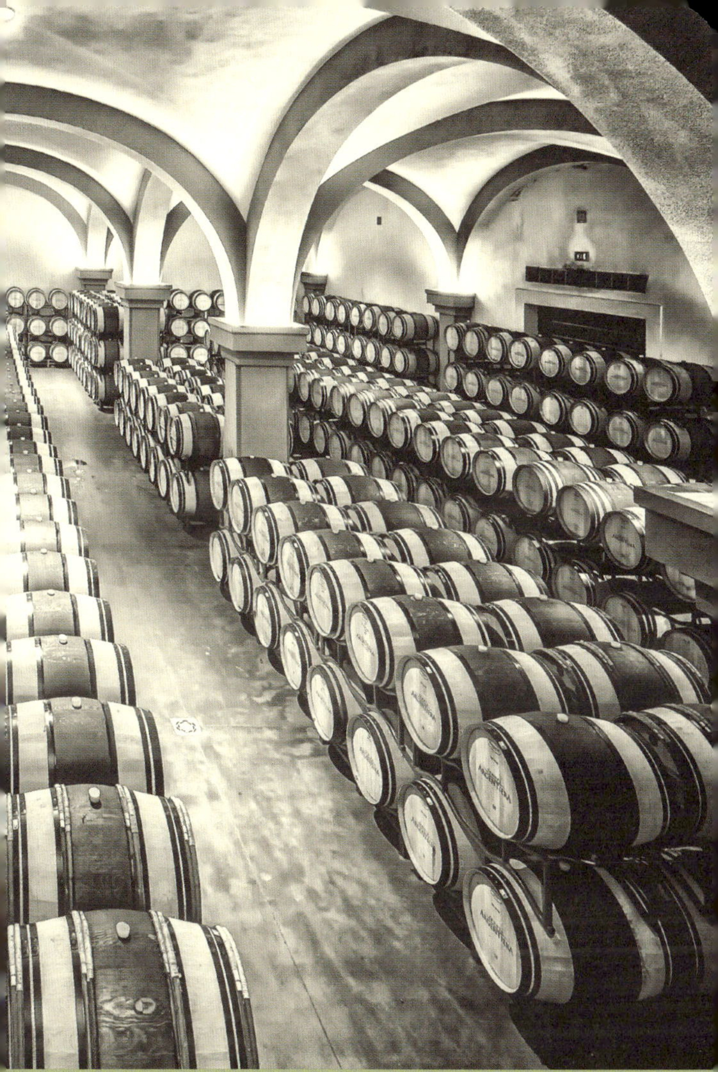

il resto. Con l'aiuto dell'enologo Giacomo Tachis nacque il Sassicaia ed a ruota tutti i più famosi vini DOC di Bolgheri. La Tenuta Argentiera, dove si mischiano viti, querce, olivi e pini marittimi, è nata nel 1999 e si trova a Donoratico, molto vicino al mare.

* See end pages for German and English translation

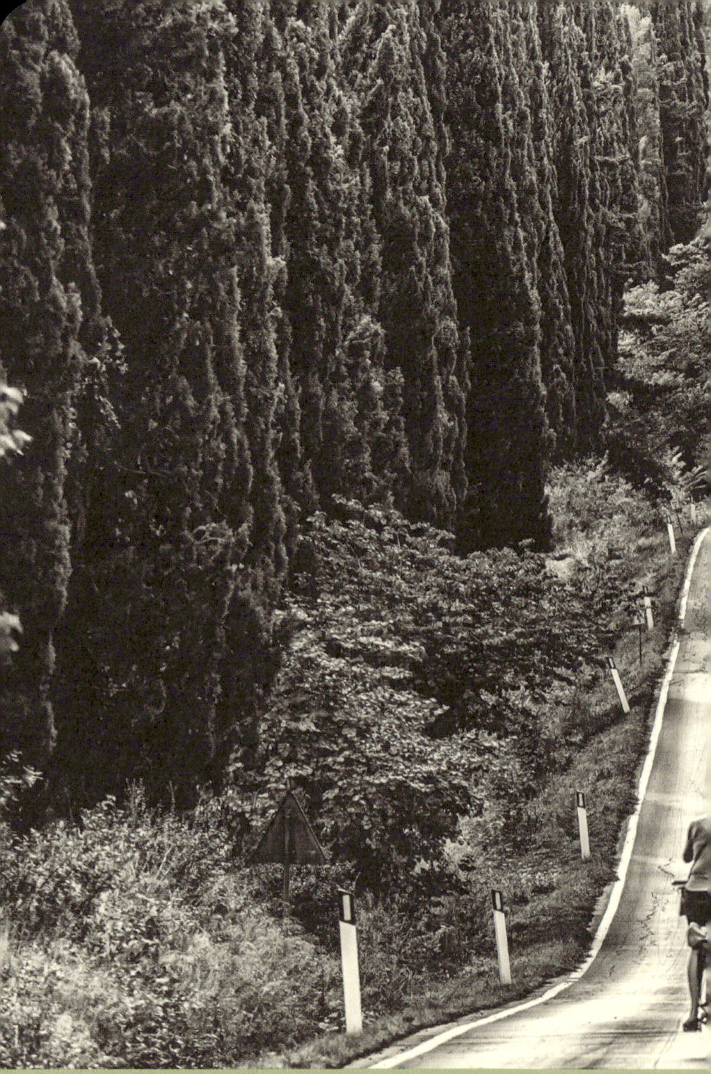

31

I cipressi di Bolgheri

"I cipressi che a Bólgheri alti e schietti
Van da San Guido in duplice filar,
Quasi in corsa giganti giovinetti
Mi balzarono incontro e mi guardar..."
(Giosuè Carducci, Davanti San Guido, 1885)

* See end pages for German and English translation

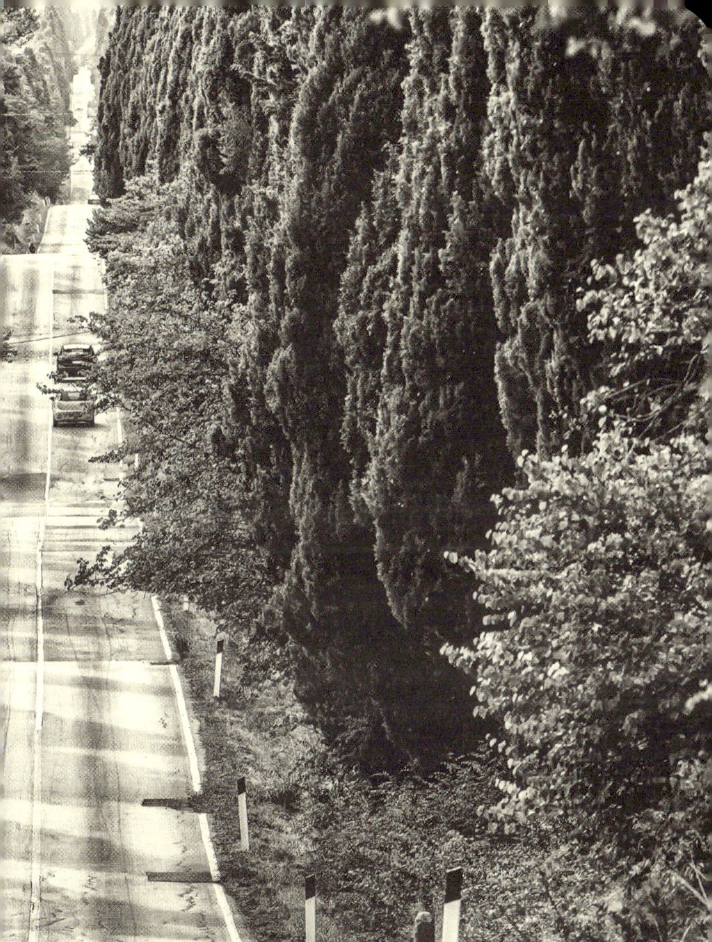

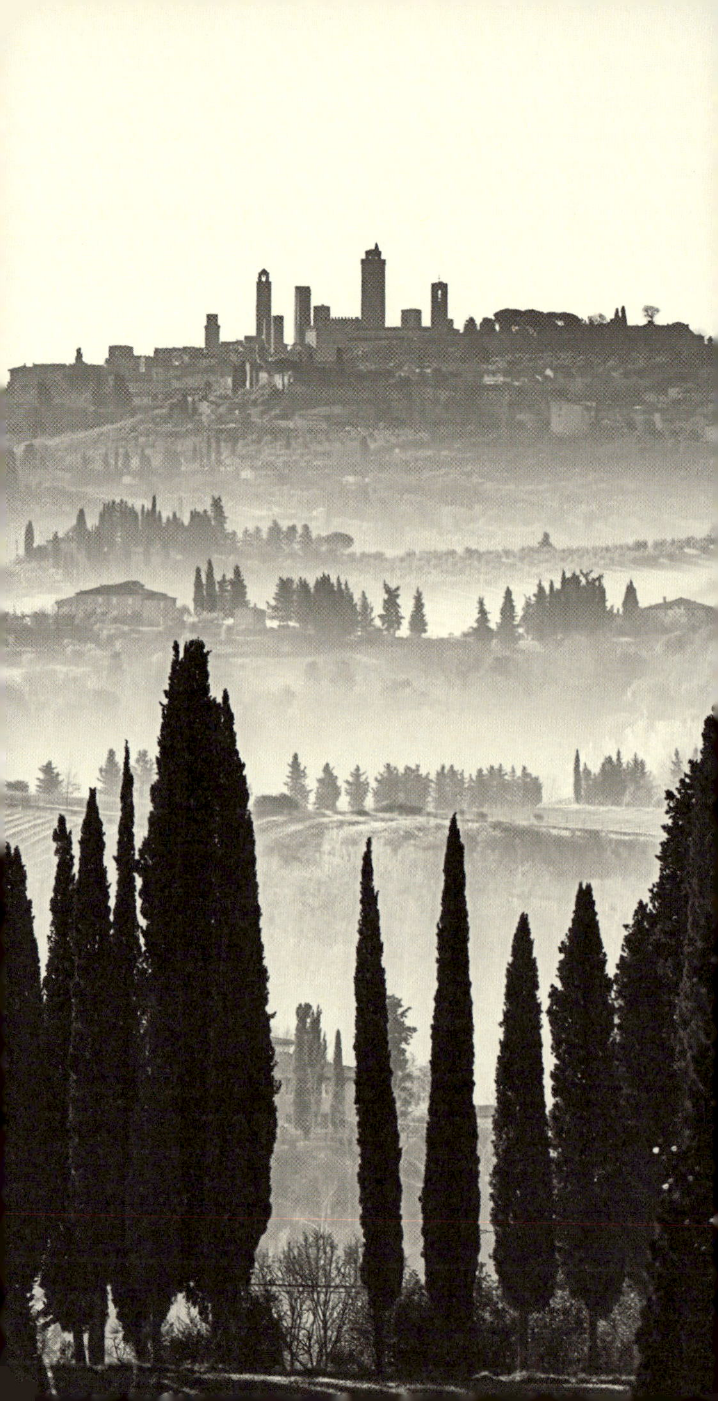

32

Cipressi a San Gimignano

Al di sopra dei cipressi e delle colline si erge il profilo di San Gimignano, forse il borgo più famoso della Toscana. La sua fama si deve soprattutto alle torri. In epoca medievale erano 72, oggi ne restano 14. La più antica è la Torre Rognosa, dell'inizio del XIII secolo; la più alta la Torre Grossa con i suoi 54 metri.

* See end pages for German and English translation

33

Struzzi Metropolitani

L'opera "Struzzi Metropolitani" di Yu Zhaoyang si trova lungo la strada comunale di Catignano tra Pievasciata e Ponte a Bozzone e fa parte del Parco Sculture del Chianti. Originariamente le figure guardavano nelle finestre di un grattacielo, ora quasi si nascondono timidamente dietro due cipressi: un passaggio repentino dal metropolitano al bucolico che le due figure avranno certamente apprezzato.

* See end pages for German and English translation

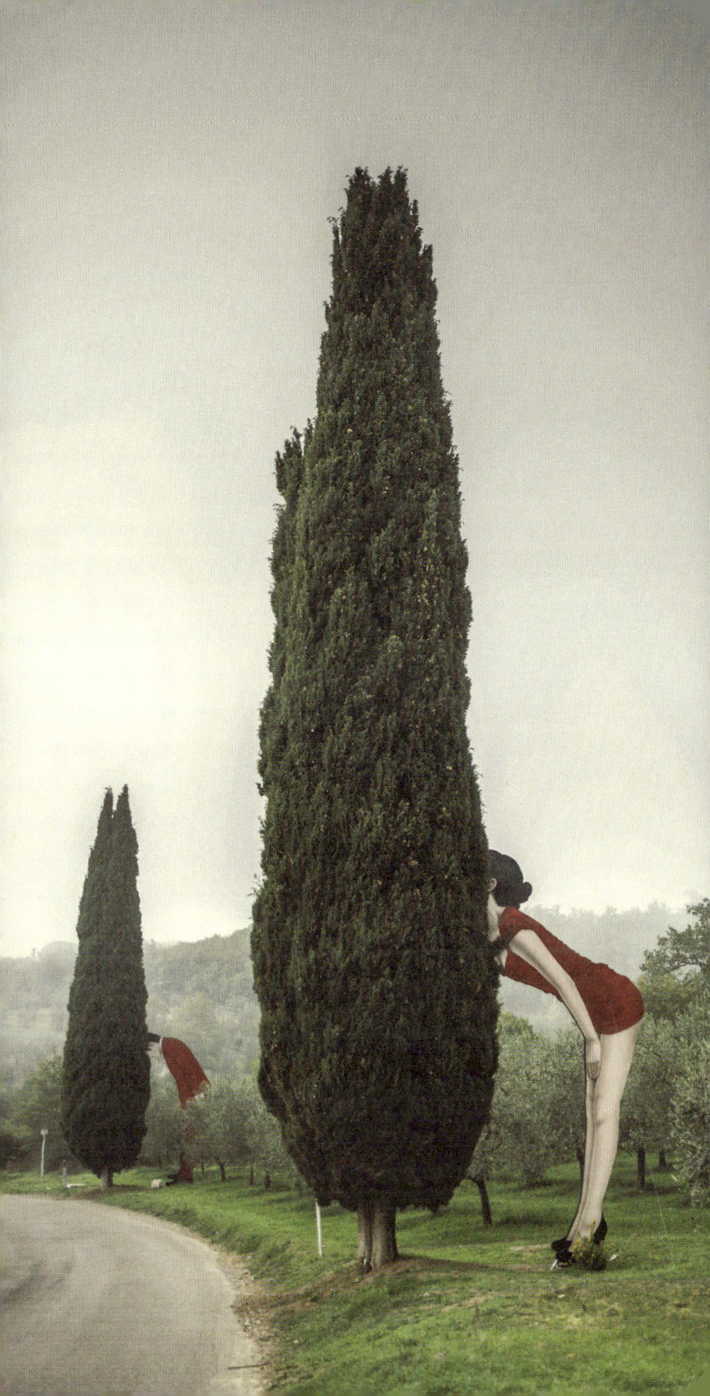

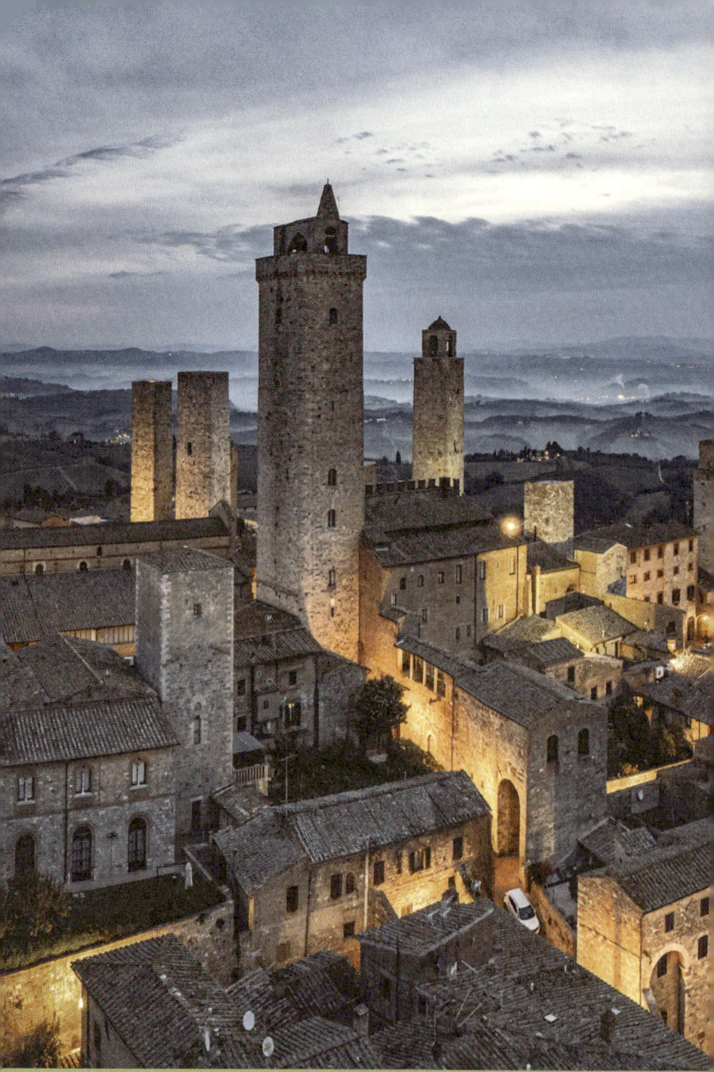

34

San Gimignano
Ai più forse i nomi di "Ezio Auditore" e di "Assassin's Creed" non diranno molto, ma gli appassionati non avranno certo dimenticato una pietra miliare dei videogiochi datata 2009. In una trama fantasiosa e piena di inesattezze il protagonista del videogioco Ezio Auditore scala

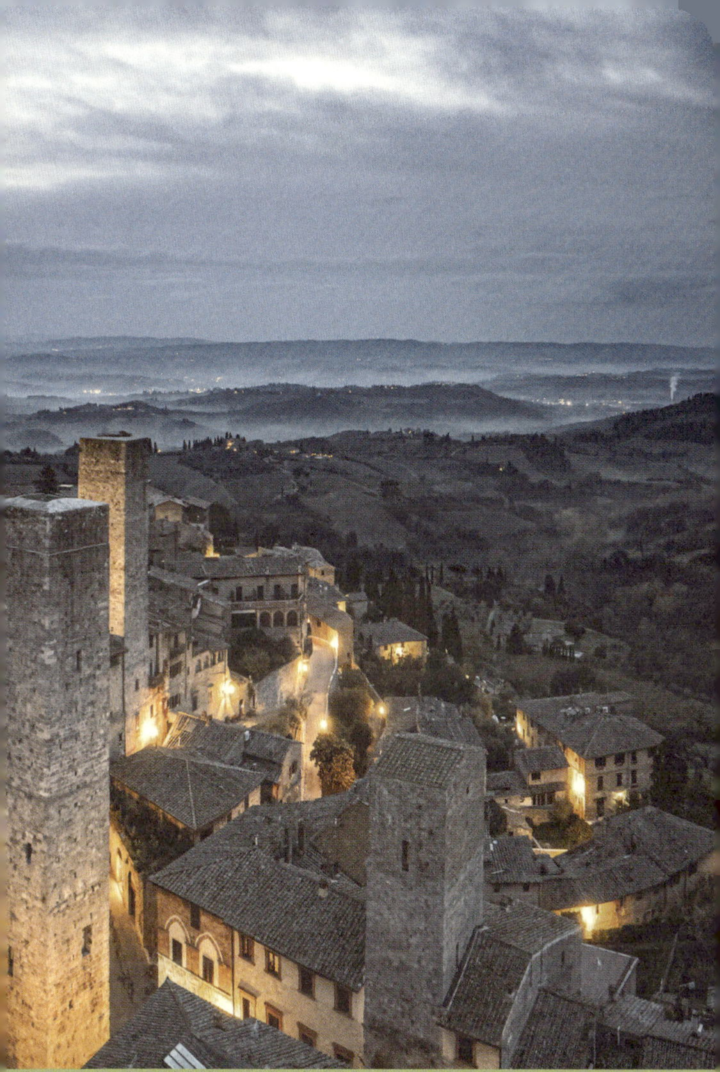

la Torre Grossa di San Gimignano per poi stabilire la sua dimora in una villa poco fuori Monteriggioni. Incredibile a dirsi ma il videogioco divenne così famoso da aumentare la presenza turistica nella zona...

* See end pages for German and English translation

35

Cappella dei Pazzi

L'architettura rinascimentale, prendendo spunto dai classici greci, si basava su moduli, che ripetuti più volte, davano equilibrio ed eleganza agli edifici secondo le leggi della prospettiva appena scoperte. Andrea de' Pazzi, nobile famiglia di ricchi mercanti fiorentini, commissionò la cappella commemorativa di famiglia a Brunelleschi. Il modulo scelto dal famoso architetto era il diametro della cupola, che doveva essere uguale all'altezza dei muri e alla larghezza dell'ambiente: geometricamente un cubo sormontato da una semisfera. Si dovevano aggiungere le due ali laterali coperte a botte e la scarsella dell'altare, con dimensioni di un quinto del modulo. Ci si rifaceva molto alla Sagrestia Vecchia in San Lorenzo, ma non nella decorazione dell'ambiente affidata a Luca della Robbia e non a Donatello, con il quale Brunelleschi – sostenitore della superiorità dell'architettura su scultura e pittura – aveva litigato a morte. La cappella non servì molto ai Pazzi: nel 1478 la Congiura dei Pazzi cambiò gli equilibri della Firenze rinascimentale a favore dei Medici, eliminando quasi tutti i membri della famiglia.

* See end pages for German and English translation

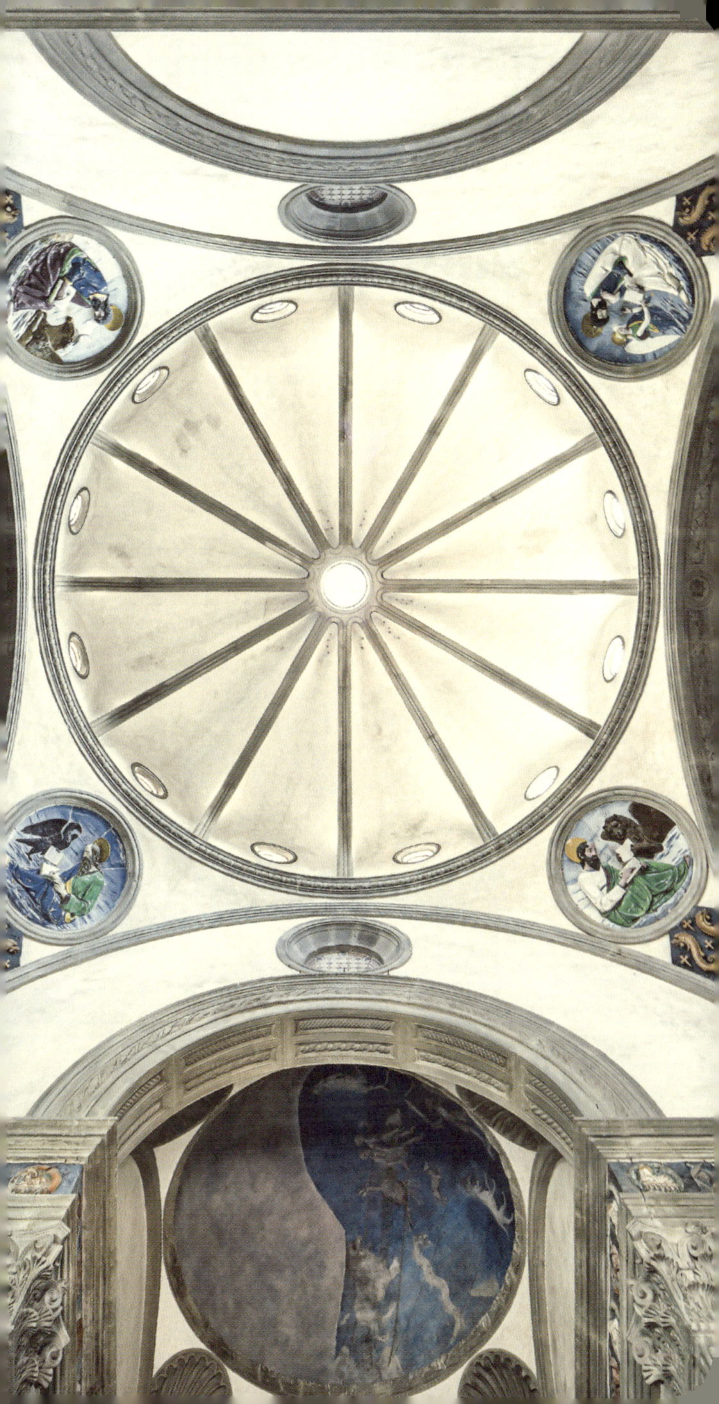

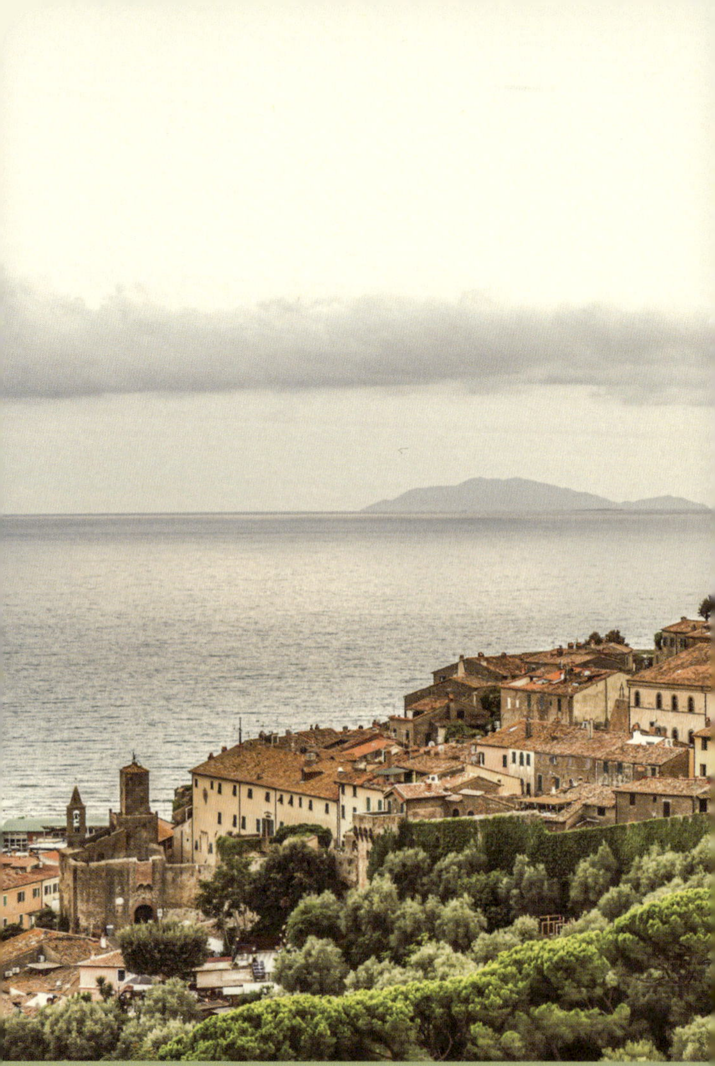

36

Castiglione della Pescaia

"...al castello d'argento di tre torri, sormontate da tre crescenti montanti dello stesso." Dimenticando i Pisani che costruirono il castello, lo stemma comunale ricorda i dominatori prima della nascita del Granducato di Toscana: i Piccolomini – i tre spicchi di luna – e gli Aragonesi – le tre torri. In pochi ricordano invece che nel cimitero-

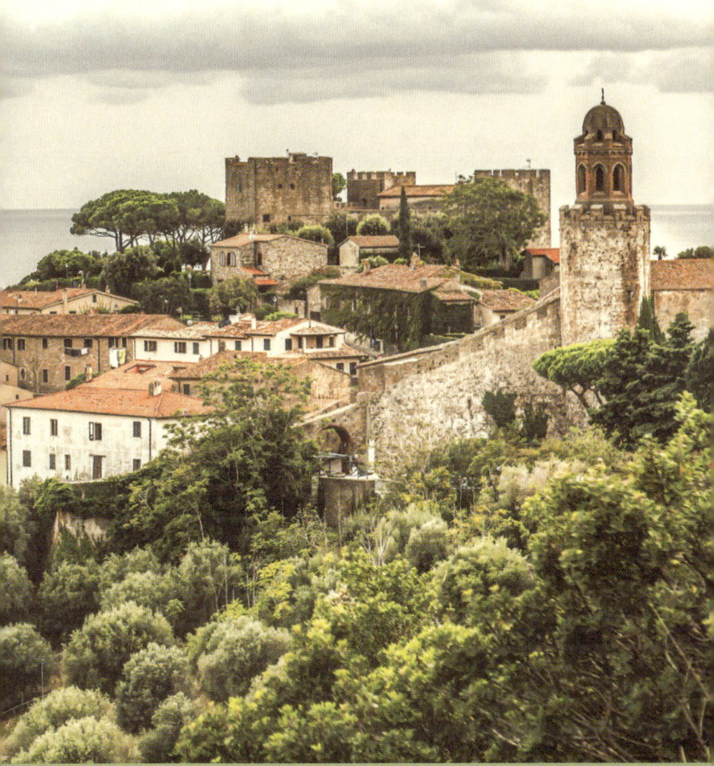

giardino di Castiglione della Pescaia, nella pineta di Roccamare, è sepolto Italo Calvino, che scelse – colpito – la località balneare maremmana come "buen retiro" dal 1972.

* See end pages for German and English translation

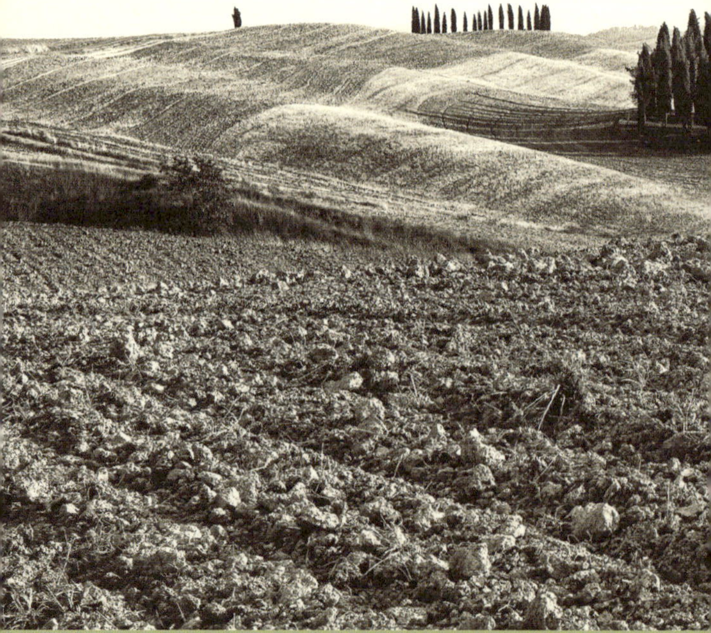

37

Cipressi di San Quirico d'Orcia

Sembrano essere nati come "roccolo di caccia", un boschetto di alberi creato dai cacciatori per attirare gli uccelli e poi catturarli con le reti. Ora i cipressi di San Quirico sono un vero e proprio simbolo della Val d'Orcia, al pari di Pienza e Bagno Vignoni. Sono fra i 55 alberi monumentali protetti dalla Regione Toscana.

* See end pages for German and English translation

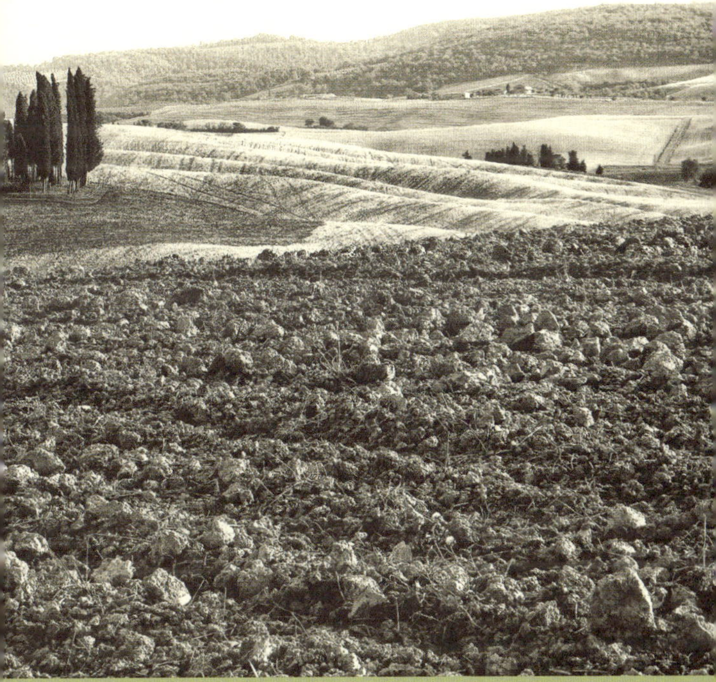

1 **Der David und die Kuppel**

Nachdem der David im Jahr 1504 fertiggestellt und übergeben worden war, stellte sich für die Stadt Florenz die Frage, wohin nun mit der Statue? Wir befinden uns in der Zeit der zweiten Republik Florenz und die Figur des David gewann eine tiefgreifende symbolische Bedeutung. Denn wie einst David Goliath, sollte die junge Republik alle finsteren Mächte überwinden.

Rasch wurde klar, dass die ursprünglich geplante Positionierung auf den Apsidenpfeilern der Kathedrale keine adäquate Wahl darstellte. Eine Bürgerdebatte wurde initiiert und eine Kommission ins Leben gerufen, bestehend aus herausragenden Künstlern jener prägenden Epoche – darunter Größen wie Botticelli, Filippino Lippi, Leonardo da Vinci, il Perugino, Giuliano da Sangallo und Andrea della Robbia. Nach intensiver Beratung fiel die Wahl auf den Vorschlag von Filippino Lippi: Die Statue sollte neben dem Eingang des Palazzo Vecchio positioniert werden. Seit mehr als fünf Jahrhunderten ermöglicht diese Entscheidung, die beiden prominentesten Symbole von Florenz – den David und den Dom – auf einen Blick zu erfassen.

2 **Die Ponte Vecchio in Florenz**

Die Ponte Vecchio in Florenz hat so einiges erlebt. In der Nacht vom dritten auf den vierten August 1944 zerstörten die sich zurückziehenden Nazis während des Zweiten Weltkriegs alle Brücken der Stadt, außer der Ponte Vecchio. Der deutsche Konsul Gerhard Wolf konnte ihre Zerstörung verhindern, indem er betonte, welchen Charme die florentinische Brücke auf Adolf Hitler während seines Besuchs im Jahr 1938 ausgeübt hatte. Am 4. November 1966 traf die Stadt eine schlimme Überschwemmung, die heftigste ihrer Geschichte. Die Ponte Vecchio glich einem Schilfrohr im Fluss Arno, das Wasser flutete die flachen Brückenbögen und die unteren Stockwerk der Geschäfte waren überschwemmt. Obwohl anschließend mitgenommen, schmutzig, zerstört und gespickt mit feststeckenden Bäumen, hielt die Ponte Vecchio stand. Damit wurde ihr Mythos als unzerstörbare Brücke endlich geboren.

3 **Die Zypressen von Monticchiello**

Man sagt, die Toskana sei das Land der Oliven, Weinberge und Zypressen. Letztere haben Landschaft tiefgehend geprägt: Die Natur oder eine göttliche Hand hat sie genau dort platziert, wo sie sein sollten - wie es in Monticchiello der Fall ist.

4 **Der Steinbruch Nummer 84 von Ravaccione**

Nach der Meinung zahlreicher Bildhauer wird zwischen Ravaccione und Fantiscritti seit jeher feinstes Carrara-Marmor von überragender Qualität abgebaut. Die Steinbrüche, die seit der Römerzeit im Tagebau betrieben werden, haben im Laufe der Jahrhunderte das beeindruckende Panorama der Apuanischen Alpen geformt. Im Jahr 1963 gab es jedoch einen entscheidenden Wendepunkt, als Carlo Dell'Amico die Ausgrabungstechnik von innen erfand: Ausgehend Ausgehend vom Tunnel der Marmifera, einer stillgelegten Eisenbahnlinie zum Marmortransport, grub er gigantische Hohlräume von 24000 Kubikmetern. Von imposanten Säulen gestützt gleichen sie schimmernden Kathedralen, in denen jegliches Gefühl für Zeit und Proportion verloren geht.

5 **Via Fillungo in Lucca**

Flaniert man durch Lucca, ist es fast unmöglich, die Via Fillungo nicht zu kreuzen. Meist geschieht dies ganz zufällig. Auf einer Länge von 700 Metern durchquert diese die Stadt von der mittelalterlichen Porta dei Borghi bis hin zur Via Santa Croce, vorbei an der Piazza dell'Anfiteatro und der Kirche San Frediano. Auf ihrem letzten Abschnitt, welcher dem römischen Kardinalweg folgt, trifft man auf die Kirche San Cristoforo und den Torre delle Ore. An diesem Ort kann man dem Geist von Lucida Mansi begegnen, die einst ihre Seele an den Teufel verkaufte, um dreißig Jahre lang jung und schön zu bleiben. Nach Ablauf dieser Zeit kletterte sie auf den Turm, um die Uhr und somit den Lauf der Zeit anzuhalten. Da ihr das natürlich nicht gelang, musste sie ihren Preis dafür zahlen.

6 **Brunelleschis Kuppel**

Messer Filippo stand vor einem Zylinder von 77 Braccia (floreninisches Längenmaß), also 45 Meter Breite und 55 Meter Höhe, der von einer Kuppel bedeckt werden sollte. Mit anderen Worten: Hier sollte die größte Kuppel der Welt entstehen. Lange Zeit wurde Brunelleschi von den Florentinern als „Esel" verspottet und beschimpft, weil er ein so innovatives Projekt präsentierte, dass es beinahe das Unglaubliche berührte: Es sah weder hölzerne Verstärkungen noch Rippen vor, denn diese hätten das Gewicht der Kuppel nicht aushalten können und obendrein ein Vermögen gekostet. Nein, Brunelleschis Plan sah eine selbsttragende Mauerwerkstechnik vor, welche aus Ziegeln bestand, die in einer 'Fischgräten'-Formation angeordnet waren und so zwei konzentrische Kuppeln bildeten. Anscheinend wurden die Ziegel direkt auf der Baustelle gebrannt und hatten alle eine unregelmäßige Form, um dem Mauerwerk die richtige Neigung für das Schließen der Kuppel geben zu können. Die Kathedrale Santa Maria del Fiore wurde 1436 schließlich eingeweiht, damals noch ohne Laterne. Bis heute ist ihre Kuppel die größte der Welt, die jemals aus Kalk und Ziegeln gebaut wurde.

7 **Der schiefe Turm von Pisa**

Zweifellos eines der symbolträchtigsten Denkmäler Italiens auf der ganzen Welt. Seine charakteristische Schräglage ist gleichzeitig Fluch und Segen, doch durch ihn ist die Piazza dei Miracoli einfach einzigartig. Er neigte sich bereits während der Bauphase, bei den Arbeiten am dritten Ring. Im Laufe der Jahrhunderte wurde der Turm mehrfach untersucht und restauriert. Es gab sogar Versuche, ihn wieder aufzurichten. Viele Einheimische haben übrigens die 276 Stufen bis zu seiner Spitze nie selbst erklommen. Der lokale Aberglaube besagt, dass es Pech bringt!

8 **Insel Elba und Sant'Andrea**

Vom Capo Sant'Andrea ziehen sich glatte Granitfelsen, von den Elbanern „Cote Piane" genannt, bis hinunter zum Strand, wo, ohne sich um das kristallklare Wasser zu kümmern einst Schiffe aller Art anlegten. Jedoch nicht, um Eisenerz, sondern den auf den Terrassen der Gegend produzierten Wein zu laden.

9 **Piazza Anfiteatro (Die Arena von Lucca)**

In der Flavischen Ära mit Sesterzen – römische Münzen – des Bürgers Quintus Vibius erbaut, hatte das Amphitheater von Lucca eine klassische Ellipsenform, und konnte die beeindruckende Menge von 10.000 Zuschauer fassen. Im Laufe des Mittelalters wurde es nicht nur als Steinbruch zum Materialabbau genutzt, sondern diente außerdem als Salzlager, Pulvermagazin und sogar als Gefängnis. Erst im 19. Jahrhundert wurde dem Amphitheater neues Leben eingehaucht: Der Architekt Lorenzo Nottolini konzentrierte sich dabei ausschließlich auf die Gebäude am äußeren Rand. Auf diese Weise entstand einer der einzigartigsten Plätze Italiens, der viel Geschichte in seinen steinernen Mauern trägt.

10 **Die Piazza di Greve in Chianti**

In der Toskana nennt man die Plätze, auf denen Märkte stattfinden, „mercatali“. Über den Markt von Greve in Chianti wurde erstmals im 13. Jahrhundert berichtet. An der Strecke von Florenz nach Siena gelegen, galt er als der bedeutendste im gesamten Chianti-Gebiet. Heute findet dieser historische Markt jeden Samstag statt. Zusammen mit den nahegelegenen Geschäften, Metzgereien und Restaurants unter den charmanten Arkaden dieses Platzes, ist er noch heute eine echte Attraktion.

11 **Mascagni-Terrasse**

In manchen Momenten des Tages erinnert sie geradezu an ein surrealistisches Gemälde von Salvador Dalì. Mit ihren 38.000 schwarzen und weißen Fliesen und den 4.000 Säulen des Geländers ist sie der stimmungsvollste Ort Livornos, ein Aussichtspunkt mit atemberaubendem Blick auf die Schönheit und Weite des Meeres.

12 **Der Dom von Siena**

Als die Stadt im 14. Jahrhundert immer mehr aufblühte und ihr Ansehen wuchs, beschloss man, eine neue Kathedrale zu bauen, die der Stadt besonderen Glanz verleihen sollte. Das Vorhaben war beeindruckend und die (Kathedrale) von heute besteht nur aus dem Querschiff, das das einzige realisierte Teilstück des ursprünglichen Plans darstellt. Leider wurde das Projekt wegen struktureller Probleme und vor allem aufgrund der Pest, welche die Stadt im Jahr 1348 heimsuchte, nie zu Ende gebracht. Als stummer Zeuge dieser Ambitionen bleibt uns die „Facciatone“, die enorme Fassade, deren schiere Größe die ursprüngliche Vision nur erahnen lässt. Dennoch wurde die Kathedrale später prachtvoll vollendet und gilt als eines der besten Beispiele für die romanisch-gotische Architektur Italiens.

13 **Bagno Vignoni**

Man braucht nicht viel Vorstellungskraft, sich Lorenzo, den Prächtigen oder Papst Pius II. auf der Piazza delle Sorgenti – dem Platz der Quellen – in Bagno Vignoni vorzustellen. Das dortige Thermalbad an der Via Francigena war damals sehr beliebt, den hier sprudelten Schwefelquellen von angenehmen 49 Grad, denen heilende Kräfte zugeschrieben wurden. Allerdings besagt die Legende, dass Lapa, die Mutter der zukünftigen Heiligen Katharina von Siena, darüber nicht besonders glücklich war - und vielleicht war das sogar gut so. Sie brachte ihre Tochter hierhin in der Hoffnung, dass die Weltlichkeit des Ortes sie von der Idee abbringen würde, Nonne zu werden...

14 **Luminara von San Ranieri - Rainer von Pisa**
Schon seit dem Mittelalter wurde San Ranieri von der Pisaner Landbevölkerung hoch verehrt. In Anbetracht eines fehlenden Fingers an seinem Skelett, angeblich aufgrund eines Käsediebstahls vor seiner Zeit als Eremit, wurde ihm als „heiligen Dieb" gehuldigt. Gegen Ende des 17. Jahrhunderts wurde der Körper von Ranieri degli Scaccieri in einen neuen Schrein im Dom von Pisa verlegt, ein zweifellos prestigeträchtigerer Ort für den bereits offiziellen Schutzpatron der Stadt. Um ebendiesen zu feiern, wurde die Stadt traditionell mit Tausenden von Kerzen beleuchtet. Früher malten die Lichter der Kerzen phantasievolle Bilder entlang des Flussufers. Heutzutage folgt die Beleuchtung den Konturen der Gebäude, ergänzt von kreativen Dekorationen. Am Ende der Feierlichkeiten wartet ein spektakuläres Feuerwerk.

15 **Palazzo Vecchio, Florenz**
Ein bewundernswertes Beispiel für die zivile Architektur des 14. Jahrhunderts ist der Palazzo dei Priori oder auch Palazzo della Signoria. Er erhielt den Beinamen „Vecchio", als Eleonora di Toledo im Jahr 1550 den Palazzo Pitti erwarb und dort die neue Residenz der Medici einrichtete. Bemerkenswert ist der majestätische Arnolfo-Turm, der vom Hauptgebäude abweicht. Mit einer Höhe von 94 Metern wurde er auf einem bereits vorhandenen Turm namens „Torre della Vacca" errichtet, welcher der Familie Foraboschi gehörte. Der Turm steht deshalb direkt auf dem Boden und ist nicht die Struktur des Palazzos integriert.

16 **Giugno Pisano**
Während des Giugno Pisano finden in Pisa eine Reihe von Veranstaltungen zu Ehren des städtischen Schutzpatrons, San Ranieri, statt. Besonders hervorzuheben sind das Gioco del Ponte – das Brückenspiel, die Regata di San Ranieri – die Regatta – und die Luminara di San Ranieri – das Lichterfest. Bei Sonnenuntergang am letzten Samstag im Juni führt der historische Umzug mit beeindruckenden 709 Teilnehmern zum Gioco del Ponte, bei dem die Stadtviertel Tramontana und Mezzogiorno in einem Kräftemessen auf der Brücke Ponte di Mezzo gegeneinander antreten.

17 **Rotes Haus von Ximenes**
Die „Fabbrica delle Cataratte", auch als Rotes Haus von Ximenes bekannt, wurde 1765 vom Jesuiten Leonardo Ximenes im Auftrag von Pietro Leopoldo di Lorena zur Entwässerung der Sumpflandschaft Maremma erbaut. Die primäre Aufgabe dieses Bauwerks bestand

darin, das Wasser des Padule di Castiglione von den Meeresgewässern zu separieren, da man damals glaubte, dass die Malaria durch das Vermischen von Süß- und Salzwasser entstand.

18 **Wässerfälle in Saturnia**

Laut The Guardian und der New York Times zählt die Cascata del Mulino in Saturnia zu den Dingen, die man im Leben mindestens einmal gesehen haben sollte. Von den Einheimischen liebevoll „Cascatelle"– „Wasserfällchen" genannt, entstehen sie aus den schwefelhaltigen Gewässern des Flusses Gorello. Mit einer angenehmen Temperatur von 37 Grad sind sie reich an wohltuenden Eigenschaften. Bei Kälte im Winter steigen dichte Dampfschwaden aus dem Wasser auf und verleihen dem Ort eine faszinierende Atmosphäre.

19 **Die Basilika Santa Croce**

„Schon im Vorfeld befand ich mich in einer Art Ekstase bei dem Gedanken, nach Florenz zu kommen (...) Völlig in die Betrachtung dieser erhabenen Schönheit versunken, sah ich sie aus der Nähe, berührte sie geradezu. Ich hatte jenes emotionale Stadium erreicht, in dem himmlische Empfindungen durch die Künste und leidenschaftliche Gefühle aufeinandertreffen. Beim Verlassen von Santa Croce durchfuhr mich ein Herzstich; das Leben schien für mich ausgetrocknet, ich ging und fürchtete dabei zu fallen." (Stendhal, Reise in Italien).

20 **Piazza Grande in Arezzo**

Eine der prominentesten Persönlichkeiten, die in Arezzo geboren wurden, ist zweifellos Giorgio Vasari. Im Jahr 1573 wurde die Piazza Grande vollständig umgestaltet und auf die heutigen Abmessungen reduziert, um dem herausragenden Künstler den Bau des Palazzo delle Logge zu ermöglichen. Im Gesamtbild verschmelzen die schlichten Renaissance-Linien des Palazzo auf harmonische Weise mit den bestehenden mittelalterlichen Strukturen und verleihen dem Bauensemble eine gewisse Eleganz. Im Jahr 1687 wurde dem Pöbel sogar untersagt, unter den Arkaden zu flanieren, um die Würde des Ortes zu wahren...

21 **Brunello di Montalcino - Wein**

Der Brunello di Montalcino wurde im Jahr 1865 geboren. Damals erfreute man sich eines reichlichen Wachstums dieser Reben und inzwischen ist er zu einer internationalen Qualitätsreferenz avanciert. Wegbereiter des Brunello war Clemente Santi, gefolgt von seinem Neffen Ferruccio Biondi, der den Sangiovese Grosso als geeignete Rebsorte für diesen sortenreinen Wein mit langer Reifezeit auswählte. Im Jahr 1888 wurde die erste Flasche Brunello Riserva abgefüllt. Die letzte wiederum, die geöffnet wurde, war 1994 anlässlich der Verkostung zum hundertjährigen Jubiläum.

22 **Via dei Servi**

Wenn man den Blick von der Via dei Servi aus hoch zu den unebenen Dächern schweifen lässt, offenbart sich einem die majestätische Pracht der Kuppel. Sie ist so groß, dass laut Schriftsteller Vasari während des Baus Tavernen auf den Gerüsten eingerichtet worden sind, um die Leerlaufzeiten durch das Auf- und Absteigen der Arbeiter zum Essen zu vermeiden.

23 **L'Eroica, Vintage Radrennen**
Es hätte einfach nur nach Nostalgie aussehen können: nach einer Sehnsucht nach einem Radsport, der von Schweiß, Schlamm und unbefestigten Straßen bestimmt war. Kurz gesagt: einem Radsport längst vergangener Zeiten. Stattdessen entpuppte sich die Idee von Giancarlo Brocci, eine Nischenveranstaltung zu schaffen, basierend auf längst überholten Werten, als weltweiter Erfolg. L`Eroica ist ein Retro-Radrennen mit historischen Fahrrädern und historischer Kleidung durch die wundervolle toskanische Landschaft. Sie schuf sogar Moden und neue Trends. Das Highlight: Als im Jahr 2010 eine Etappe des Giro d'Italia in Montalcino, genau auf der Strecke von l'Eroica ausgetragen wurde. Eine äußerst anspruchsvolle Etappe, im strömenden Regen... Über die Ziellinie fuhren erschöpfte, von Schlamm bedeckte Gestalten: Doch der Radsport mit seinem Zauber der Erschöpfung und der Lust am Abenteuer war wieder geboren.

24 **Piazza del Campo, Siena**
Die Piazza del Campo ist ein Platz von außergewöhnlicher Form, denn sie ist schneckenförmig. Der Boden besteht aus einem Fischgrätenmuster aus Ziegeln und ist durch Linien aus weißem Travertin in neun Abschnitte unterteilt. Diese Abschnitte repräsentieren einerseits die „Regierung der Neun" und gleichzeitig metaphorisch die Falten des Mantels der Jungfrau Maria. In Siena gelten die Piazza del Campo und der Palazzo Pubblico als neutrales Gebiet. Gemäß einer alten Vereinbarung gehören sie keiner der 17 Stadtteile an, in die die Stadt unterteilt ist. Aus gutem Grund findet dort der Palio statt, der Wettkampf zwischen den Stadtvierteln.

25 **Santa Maria del Fiore**
Um den Dom Santa Maria del Fiore in Florenz besser zu begreifen, ist es hilfreich, das neue Museum dell'Opera del Duomo zu besuchen. Denn seine Geschichte ist komplex und reicht vom gotischen Entwurf von Arnolfo di Cambio über den Bau von Glockenturm und Kuppel durch Giotto bis hin zu dem, was für Florenz zu einer regelrechten Saga wurde: der Fassade. Der Dom hatte zunächst eine unvollendete Fassade aus Pietraforte, die zum Teil bemalt war. Nach den üblichen heftigen Kontroversen entschied sich Florenz jedoch für das neugotische Projekt von Emilio De Fabris. Die neue Fassade wurde schließlich im Jahr 1887 eingeweiht.

26 **Der David von Michelangelo**
„Es war einmal..." – Ein König! – werden meine kleinen Leser sofort ausrufen. – „Nein, meine kleinen Leser, ihr habt euch geirrt. Es war einmal ein Stück Holz..." (Collodi, Die Abenteuer von Pinocchio, 1881-1883).
In unserem Fall könnte die Geschichte lauten: „Es war einmal ein Stück Marmor...". Denn es handelte sich um ein gewaltiges Stück minderwertigen Marmors, durchzogen von Adern und winzigen Löchern, das seit geraumer Zeit – beinahe vergessen – auf

den Baustellen des Doms stand. Nach den Auftraggebern sollte aus ihm eine imposante Statue von König David entstehen, die auf den Strebepfeilern des Doms von Florenz ihren Platz finden sollte. Bedeutende Künstler, wie im Jahr 1463-1464 Agostino di Duccio und im Jahr 1476 Antonio Rossellino hatten auf die Realisation des Projekts verzichtet. Inzwischen galt der Marmorblock als schlecht behauen und ungünstig geschnitten. Am 16. August 1501 erhielt Michelangelo schließlich den Auftrag für die beträchtliche Summe von 400 Florin. Nach etwa drei Jahren war der David geboren, und am 8. September 1504 wurde er letztlich der Stadt präsentiert: Der Eindruck, den er hinterließ, war schlichtweg überwältigend.

27 **Der Raub der Sabinerinnen**

Wir sehen drei Figuren aus Marmor: EIn alter und ein junger Mann, sowie ein Mädchen. Wir befinden uns unter der Loggia dei Lanzi in Florenz, auf der Piazza della Signoria, einem wahren Freilichtmuseum. Rasch wird klar, dass es keinen festen Standpunkt gibt, von dem aus man diese Skulptur am besten betrachtet. Stattdessen enthüllen sich beim Annähern, Umkreisen und Entfernen stets neue Details, Verflechtungen und Perspektiven... Dieses Kunstwerk, „Der Raub der Sabinerinnen" genannt, gilt als das wohl bedeutendste Meisterwerk der manieristischen Skulptur und stammt aus den Händen des Flamen Jean de Boulogne, der in Florenz auch als Giambologna bekannt ist.

28 **Baratti**

Es ist nicht ganz leicht, die Magie eines Ortes in Worte zu fassen. Die Empfindungen, die er weckt, sind zart, subjektiv, in sich selbst verschlossen. Der Golf von Baratti mit seinem goldenen Sandstrand und dem ihn umgebenden Pinienwald ist zweifelsohne ein bezaubernder Ort, der ein einzigartiges Flair verströmt. Hier scheint die Zeit nach einem ganz eigenen Takt zu verstreichen. Selbst im Sommer entleert sich die Szenerie beinahe unerklärlich mit Einbruch der Dunkelheit und schenkt dem Besucher dabei wundervolle Momente. Ein Phänomen, das sich auch in der Nebensaison häufig findet. Die Gegend präsentiert sich geradezu verlassen, und der Aufstieg zur Rocca di Populonia offenbart die bezaubernden Düfte der mediterranen Macchia sowie atemberaubende Panoramen.

29 **Torre del Mangia**

„Il Mangia" – ein Spitzname – „Der Esser" - muss in den Tavernen von Siena seiner Zeit eine berühmte Figur gewesen sein. Wohl pflegte er dort sein ganzes Geld auszugeben. Giovanni di Duccio, so sein richtiger Name, war kurz nach 1348 der erste Glockenspieler und zeitgleich Wächter des Palazzo Civico von Siena. Der Name des Turms leitet sich folglich von seinem Spitznamen ab. Seine Tätigkeit währte jedoch nicht lange. Im Jahr 1360 schlug bereits die erste automatische Uhr die Stunden... was sich jedoch als Fehler und eine Art Rache des "Mangia" heraus stellte. Denn noch heute wird die Glocke zwar von einem Automaten geläutet, klingt aber stets ein wenig verstimmt. Nur einmal im Jahr - am Tag des Palio - wird sie von Hand geschlagen, dann ist ihr Klang jedoch perfekt...

30 **Der Keller des Weingutes Tenuta Argentiera in Bolgheri**
Die visionäre Intuition des Marchese Incisa della Rocchetta hatte sich als triumphal erwiesen: Nach seinem Ehegelübde zog er nach Bolgheri und der Marchis, inspiriert von den geliebten französischen Weinen, versuchte dort eine Sorte Cabernet anzupflanzen, die bereits in Migliarino in der Nähe von Pisa gut gedieh. Die Meeresnähe war dabei sehr zuträglich. Mit der kundigen Unterstützung des Önologen Giacomo Tachis wurde schließlich der Sassicaia geboren, gefolgt von den renommiertesten Weinen mit kontrollierter Herkunftsbezeichnung (DOC) Bolgheri. Das Landgut Argentiera, ein Ort, an dem sich Reben, Eichen, Oliven und Küstenpinien harmonisch vereinen, wurde im Jahr 1999 ins Leben gerufen und befindet sich in der Nähe von Donoratico, in unmittelbarer Nähe der Küste.

31 **Die Zypressen von Bolgheri**
„Hoch und aufrecht
gehen die Zypressen in doppelter Reihe
von San Guido nach Bólgheri,
wie riesige Jungen, fast rennend,
eilen sie mir entgegen, um nach mir zu sehen."
(Giosuè Carducci, Davanti San Guido, 1885)

32 **Die Zypressen in San Gimignano**
Über den sanften Hügeln und den Zypressen erhebt sich die elegante Silhouette von San Gimignano, zweifellos eines der malerischsten Dörfer in der Toskana. Sein Ruhm ist eng mit den markanten Türmen verbunden. Im Mittelalter ragten hier stolze 72 Türme empor, von denen heute noch 14 majestätisch in den Himmel streben. Der älteste unter ihnen ist der Torre Rognosa aus dem frühen 13. Jahrhundert. Der imposanteste ist jedoch der Torre Grossa, der ganze 54 Meter hoch ist.

33 **Großstadtstrauße**
Das Kunstwerk „Struzzi Metropolitani" – „Großstadtstrausse" von Yu Zhaoyang befindet sich entlang der Gemeindestraße von Catignano zwischen Pievasciata und Ponte a Bozzone und ist Teil des Skulpturenparks Chianti. Ursprünglich schauten die Figuren aus den Fenstern eines Wolkenkratzers, doch mittlerweile verbergen sie sich beinahe schüchtern hinter zwei Zypressen. Den abrupten Wechsel von der Großstadt zum Ländlichen haben sie sicherlich zu schätzen gewusst.

34 **San Gimignano**
Den meisten mögen die Namen Ezio Auditore und Assassin's Creed nicht viel sagen, doch eingefleischten Fans bleibt der Meilenstein der Videospiele aus dem Jahr 2009 sicher unvergesslich: In einer phantasievollen Handlung, wenn auch mit einigen Ungenauigkeiten, erklimmt der Protagonist des Videospiels, Ezio Auditore, den Turm Torre Grossa von San Gimignano, um anschließend seinen Wohnsitz in einer Villa in der Nähe von Monteriggioni zu begründen. Erstaunlicherweise führte dieses Videospiel sogar zu einem Anstieg des Tourismus in der Region.

35 Pazzi-Kapelle

In Anlehnung an die klassischen Griechen griff die Renaissance-Architektur auf Elemente zurück, die den Gebäuden durch ihre geschickte Wiederholung Gleichgewicht und Eleganz verliehen, und zwar gemäß den kürzlich entdeckten Gesetzen der Perspektive. Der wohlhabende florentinische Händler Andrea de' Pazzi, inspiriert von dieser Bewegung, beauftragte den herausragenden Architekten Brunelleschi mit dem Bau einer Gedenkkapelle für seine Familie.
Brunelleschi, ein Verfechter der Überlegenheit der Architektur gegenüber Skulptur und Malerei, wählte den Durchmesser der Kuppel als grundlegendes Element. Dieser sollte harmonisch der Höhe der Wände und der Breite des Raums entsprechen, sodass geometrisch betrachtet ein Kubus entstand, überdacht von einer Halbkugel. Um die Kapelle zu vervollständigen, wurden zwei seitliche Flügel mit Tonnengewölben und die Altar-Apsis hinzugefügt, deren Maße einem Fünftel des Bauelements entsprachen.
Man orientierte sich stark an der Alten Sakristei der Basilika di San Lorenzo, allerdings nicht hinsichtlich der Dekoration des Innenraumes, die Luca della Robbia anvertraut wurde und nicht Donatello, mit dem Brunelleschi – ein Befürworter der Überlegenheit der Architektur über Skulptur und Malerei – bis aufs Äußerste zerstritten war. Bedauerlicherweise währte die Kapelle der Familie Pazzi nicht lange. Im Jahr 1478 erschütterte die Verschwörung der Pazzi das Gleichgewicht des florentinischen Renaissance-Zeitalters, indem sie zugunsten der Medici wirkte und nahezu alle Mitglieder der Familie auslöschte.

36 Castiglione della Pescaia

„ ...an der silbernen Burg mit drei Türmen, überragt von drei Halbmonden, die an ihm emporsteigen". Das Wappen der Stadt erinnert nicht etwa an die Pisaner, die immerhin die Erbauer des Schlosses waren, sondern an die Herrscher vor der Gründung des Großherzogtums der Toskana: Nämlich einerseits an die Piccolomini – verkörpert durch die drei Mondsichel-Elemente – und andererseits an die Aragonesen – repräsentiert durch die drei Türme. Nur wenige erinnern sich jedoch daran, dass im Gartenfriedhof von Castiglione della Pescaia, gelegen im Pinienhain von Roccamare, Italo Calvino beerdigt ist. Der renommierte Schriftsteller wählte diesen Badeort in der Maremma seit 1972 als seinen „Buen Retiro" – seinen Ort der Ruhe und Erholung.

37 Die Zypressen von San Quirico d'Orcia

Sie scheinen als Jagdtaubenschlag entstanden zu sein: Ein Hain von Bäumen, den Jäger angelegt haben, um darin anschließend Vögel zu fangen. Heute sind die Zypressen von San Quirico ein charakteristisches Symbol des Val d'Orcia. Auch Pienza und Bagno Vignoni sind durch sie unverkennbar. Sie gehören zu den 55 geschützten Baumarten der Region Toskana.

1 **David and the "Cupolone"**

When David was presented to Florence in 1504, the city struggled to decide where to place the sculpture. In this period of the Second Republic, the David statue held special symbolic significance: the young republic would defeat unjust powers, much as biblical David did against Goliath. It quickly became clear that the intended location on the buttresses of the Duomo's apse was unsuitable. Amidst hot civic debate, a commission was established to decide the best placement for the statue. The committee included prominent artists of the day: Botticelli, Filippino Lippi, Leonardo da Vinci, Perugino, Giuliano da Sangallo, and Andrea della Robbia. In the end, Filippino Lippi's proposal won out, dignifying the statue's placement at the entrance of the Palazzo Vecchio. For more than five centuries, their decision has allowed visitors to Florence to encapsulate the two most important symbols of Florence in a single glance: The David and the "Cupolone" (dome of the Florence Cathedral).

2 **The Ponte Vecchio in Florence**

In Florence they say Ponte Vecchio stands with them through the good times and the hard. In August 1944 as the Nazis retreated, they destroyed all the city bridges over the Arno. All but the Ponte Vecchio, for German Consul Gerhard Wolf prevented its destruction by referencing Adolf Hitler's fascination with the wonderful bridge during his 1938 visit to Florence. On November 4th, 1966, yet another flood overwhelmed Florence, the most devastating ever. Ponte Vecchio was like a twig at the water's mercy as the Arno rose over its arches to flood the lower floors of the shops. As the water receded, the bridge emerged: battered, chipped and dirty, the shops ruined. Trees and driftwood were lodged everywhere, but the bridge still stood, testament to the myth that the Ponte Vecchio was built indestructible.

3 **The Cypress Trees of Monticchiello**

Everyone knows Tuscany is a land of olive groves, vineyards, and cypress trees and the cypress trees are iconic features of the landscape: each one positioned exactly where it should be, by nature or by a divine hand, perfectly, as they are in in Monticchiello.

4 **Cava Ravaccione n. 84**

Most sculptors agree that Carrara marble from the quarries of Ravaccione and Fantiscrive is of exquisite quality. The quarry workings have been open-air since Roman times, a landmark feature of the Apuan Alps, but Carlo Dell'Amico turned tradition on its head in 1963, when he invented the internal excavation technique. Starting from the Marmifera tunnel (a disused railway once used to transport the marble, gigantic caves of 24,000 cubic meters were dug: immense glittering cathedrals, inside which all sense of time and proportion is lost.

5 **The Via Fillungo in Lucca**

In Lucca, it's impossible to miss Via Fillungo. You'll come across it for sure, even by random chance. Stretching 700 meters, it traverses the city from the medieval Porta dei Borghi to Via Santa Croce, skirting Piazza dell'Anfiteatro and the Church of San Frediano. In its final stretch - the part that follows the Roman cardo – you'll find the Church of San

Cristoforo and The Clocktower where you just might encounter the ghost of Lucida Mansi on your way up. They say she sold her soul to the devil to remain young and beautiful for thirty years and when her time expired, she climbed the tower to stop the clock - and the march of time. We know she failed and paid the devil's price.

6 **Brunelleschi's Dome**

Filippo Brunelleschi found himself faced with a gigantic drum some 77 arms wide by Florentine measure (45 meters across and about 55 meters high to you and I) and it needed to be covered with a dome: the biggest in the world. His fellow Florentines laughed at him and called him an ass for his audaciously innovative project. He developed a self-supporting masonry technique based on bricks placed in a herringbone pattern and forming two concentric shells, without iron or wooden ribs (which would cost a fortune and would be too fragile to support the weight of the dome). The bricks were probably fired on-site and had an irregular shape to create the correct angle in the masonry to close the dome. The Cathedral of Santa Maria del Fiore was re-consecrated in 1436 without the lantern on top. Today, "il Duomo" remains the largest bricks-and-mortar built dome in the world.

7 **The Leaning Tower of Pisa**

Without any doubt one of the iconic monuments that represents Italy worldwide. The tower's characteristic lean has been both its torment and its fortune, giving the Piazza dei Miracoli something truly unique. The tower began to lean during construction, as the builders reached the third ring. Over the centuries since then it has been studied, restored, and "straightened" more than once. It's curious that many Pisans have never climbed the 276 steps to the top: Tradition says it would bring bad luck to those who are born and raised in Pisa.

8 **Sant'Andrea, Island of Elba**

On Capo Sant'Andrea, smooth granite rocks known by the locals as "Cote Piane" slope down to the beach where ships of all kinds once moored in the crystalline waters to carry away the wine produced on the island's terraces.

9 **Piazza dell'Anfiteatro**

Built in the Flavian era with the sesterces raised by citizen Quintus Vibio, the Lucca amphitheater had a classic elliptical shape and could seat as many as 10,000 spectators. Used as a quarry for building materials in medieval times, it was a salt warehouse and powder magazine later, and even served time as a prison. It was renovated in the 19th century by architect Lorenzo Nottolini who left only the buildings which ringed the external perimeter: thus one of the most singular squares in Italy was born.

10 **Piazza di Greve in Chianti**

In Tuscany, areas where markets are held are referred to as "mercatali" and we have reliable records of the market in Greve in Chianti from the thirteenth century. Being on the Florence-Siena route, it was the most important in the Chianti region. Today, the traditional market day is on Saturdays and is a huge attraction along with the shops, butchers, and restaurants located under the arcades of this funnel-shaped square.

11 **Terrazza Mascagni**
At certain times of the day, it might resemble a surrealistic painting by Salvador Dalì, with its 38,000 black and white tiles and its 4,000 columns. Terrazza Mascagni is the most evocative place in Livorno, an open belvedere overlooking the beauty of the sea.

12 **Siena Cathedral**
The city was flourishing, its prestige growing, and in the 14th century, Siena decided to build a new cathedral to enhance the city's splendor. The project was impressive, and the current cathedral would have formed only the transept. Unfortunately, due to structural issues and especially the Black Death that visited the city in 1348, construction ceased abruptly. What was finished is the grand outline, giving us an idea of the planned size of the building, something almost out-of-scale! Despite everything, the Cathedral was splendidly completed and is considered one of the finest examples of Italian Romanesque-Gothic architecture.

13 **Bagno Vignoni**
It isn't hard to imagine Lorenzo the Magnificent or Pope Pius II in Piazza delle Sorgenti in Bagno Vignoni. At the time, the spa was very popular because of its location on the Via Francigena and the warm sulphurous waters flowing at 49 degrees were well known for their beneficial properties. Lapa, the mother of Catherine, future Saint Catherine of Siena, brought her daughter here in hope that the worldliness of the place would cure Catherine of her desire to become a nun. It didn't work. And maybe that's a good thing!

14 **Luminara of San Ranieri**
Since the Middle Ages, San Ranieri was venerated by the people of the Pisan countryside as a saintly thief because of a missing finger in his skeleton, apparently a punishment inflicted on him for the alleged theft of a cheese before his hermitage. At the end of the 17th century, Ranieri degli Scaccieri's body was re-interred in a new reliquary in Pisa Cathedral, an appropriately prestigious resting place for the now official patron saint of the city. To celebrate, the city was lit with thousands of candles, their lights depicting fantastic buildings along the Arno. Nowadays, on June 16th each year, the lighting follows the profile of the real buildings and some more imaginative decoration and a fireworks finale.

15 **Palazzo Vecchio**
A marvelous example of 14th-century civic architecture, the Palazzo dei Priori or Palazzo della Signoria became "old" when Eleonora di Toledo purchased Palazzo Pitti in 1550 and established the Medici residence there. The majestic Arnolfo Tower is a unique feature, positioned off-center from the main body of the building. At 94 meters tall, it was built on a pre-existing tower known as "della Vacca," owned by the Foraboschi family. The Tower rises directly on the ground and not from the structure of the palace.

16 **Giugno Pisano**
During Giugno Pisano, a series of events are held in honor of the patron saint, San Ranieri. Most notable are the Gioco del Ponte (Battle of the

Bridge), the Regata di San Ranieri, and the Luminara di San Ranieri. At sunset on the last Saturday of the month, the Historical Parade of 709 participants heralds the Gioco del Ponte, where the Tramontana and Mezzogiorno districts compete in a show of strength on the Ponte di Mezzo (Middle Bridge).

17 **Casa Rossa Ximenes**
The "Waterfall Factory" was commissioned by Pietro Leopoldo di Lorena in 1765 and built by the Jesuit Leonardo Ximenes during the reclamation of the Maremma. The building's purpose was to keep the waters of the Castiglione Marshes separate from the sea because it was believed that malaria originated from the unhealthy mixing of fresh and salt waters.

18 **Mulino waterfalls in Saturnia**
According to The Guardian and The New York Times, this is a place you should visit at least once in your lifetime. The locals call them Cascatelle and they're formed by the sulphurous waters of the Gorello stream. With a temperature of 37 degrees, they're blessed with beneficial health properties. In the cold of winter, the dense clouds of steam rising from the waters make it a very evocative place.

19 **The Basilica of Santa Croce**
"I was already in a kind of ecstasy at the thought of being in Florence ...absorbed in contemplation of sublime beauty, I saw it up close; touched it, so to speak. I had reached that level of emotion where celestial sensation meets passionate feeling. Leaving Santa Croce, I had palpitations of the heart: Life had dried up for me, I walked in fear of falling." (Stendhal, Italian Journey).
The famous psychosomatic affection known as the Stendhal Syndrome or Florence Syndrome was first described at Santa Croce.

20 **Piazza Grande in Arezzo**
Giorgio Vasari is without doubt one of the most illustrious sons of Arezzo. To allow the incomparable artist to build the Palazzo delle Logge In 1573, Piazza Grande was completely renovated and reduced to its current size. The restrained Renaissance lines of the palace blend quite well with the existing medieval structures, giving the whole a certain elegance. In 1687, it was even prohibited for the ordinary townspeople to walk beneath the arcade in order to maintain its genteel decorum.

21 **Brunello di Montalcino**
The Brunello di Montalcino was first made in 1865. The growth of this wine in the last 150 years has been exponential and it has become an international reference point for quality. The pioneer of Brunello was Clemente Santi, and his nephew Ferruccio Biondi who followed him selected Sangiovese Grosso as a vine pure enough for long-term ageing. The first Brunello Riserva was bottled in 1888. The last time one was opened was in 1994 for the Centennial Tasting.

22 **Via dei Servi**
It is from Via dei Servi, looking past the irregular rooftops, that one appreciates the majesty of Brunelleschi's Dome. It's so big that

Vasari tells us that taverns were set up on the scaffolding during its construction to avoid the downtime the project would have suffered as workers descended and climbed back up after meals.

23 **The Eroica**
It could have seemed like mere nostalgia: a longing for a cycling era of mud, sweat and dirt roads – a seemingly forgotten era. It was Giancarlo Brocci's idea to create a niche event for a select few, based on values that appeared to be fading, yet has proven to be a global success, even creating a fashionable trend of its own. Its crowning moment was in 2010, when a stage of the Giro d'Italia was raced on the route of L'Eroica, finishing in Montalcino. A grueling stage, all in the rain, with exhausted riders crossing the finish line caked in mud: cycling as a triumph over adversity was rediscovered!

24 **Piazza del Campo**
This uniquely shaped piazza, often described as a "shell," is paved with herringbone-patterned terracotta and divided into 9 segments by white travertine lines. These segments represent the governors of the "Government of the Nine" and metaphorically, the folds of the Virgin Mary's cloak. In Siena, Piazza del Campo and the Palazzo Pubblico are considered neutral ground: according to an ancient agreement, they don't belong to any of the 17 districts into which the city is divided. Thus, there is no better place to race the Palio.

25 **Santa Maria del Fiore**
To properly appreciate the Cathedral of Santa Maria del Fiore in Florence you absolutely must visit the new Museo dell'Opera del Duomo. The history is complex, ranging from Arnolfo di Cambio's Gothic project to the construction of Giotto's Campanile and the Dome, leading to what was a true saga for Florence: the façade. The Cathedral had an unfinished façade in partially painted pietraforte. After the usual fierce controversies, Florence chose Emilio De Fabris's neogothic design. The façade was finally inaugurated in 1887.

26 **David of Michelangelo**
"- Once upon a time...
-There was a king!" my young readers will shout immediately.
-No, kids, you're mistaken. Once upon a time, there was a piece of wood..." (Collodi, The Adventures of Pinocchio, 1881-1883)
Not in this story. In our case, you could say, "Once upon a time, there was a piece of marble..." An enormous piece of poor-quality marble, full of veins and pocked with taroli (tiny little holes), which had been almost abandoned in the workshops of the Opera del Duomo for an age. According to the commission, it was supposed to become a statue of King David to be placed on the buttresses of the Florence Cathedral. Eminent artists of the day - Agostino di Duccio in 1463-1464 and Antonio Rossellino in 1476 had already given up on creating the work, and by then, the marble was considered "badly roughed and carved." And then Michelangelo received the commission on August 16, 1501, for the sum of 400 florins. After about three years, David was born, and on September 8, 1504, he was presented to the city: the impression he made was immense.

27 **Ratto delle Sabine**
With three marble figures - a man, a younger man, and a maiden, we are under the Loggia dei Lanzi in Piazza della Signoria, Florence, a real open-air museum. In admiring the sculpture, one notices immediately that there is no privileged point of view. By circling around, moving away and coming closer, new details, new interweavings and new perspectives are discovered. Later renamed The Rape of the Sabine Women, it is probably the masterpiece of Mannerist sculpture and the work of Flemish artist Jean de Boulogne, commonly known in Florence as Giambologna.

28 **Baratti**
It's not easy, describing a magical place. The sensations it evokes are subtle, subjective, locked within you. The Gulf of Baratti with its beach and pine forest is one such wonderful place with a unique aura. The place keeps its own time, and even in summer it inexplicably empties out at dusk, offering beautiful atmospheres. The same happens out of season: The area is practically deserted, and the climb to the Rocca di Populonia enriches you with the scents of Mediterranean scrub and breathtaking views.

29 **The Torre of Mangia**
"Il Mangia" must have been very well-known in the Sienese taverns of his time because he spent all his earnings in them! Giovanni di Duccio (his real name) was the first bell ringer and keeper of the tower of the Palazzo Pubblico in Siena shortly after 1348. The Tower takes its name from his nickname, despite him holding the job for a only a short while: He was replaced in 1360 by the city's first mechanical clock and an automaton that struck the hours...which given the troubled history of the bell, turned out to be a mistake!

30 **The cellar of Tenuta Argentiera in Bolgheri**
The intuition of Marchese Incisa della Rocchetta proved very successful! Soon after getting married, he moved to Bolgheri and, inspired by his love of French wine, he attempted to plant a variety of Cabernet found in Migliarino near Pisa. Proximity to the sea did the rest, and with the help of winemaker Giacomo Tachis, Sassicaia was born, and the most famous DOC wines of Bolgheri. Tenuta Argentiera, where vines, oak, olive trees and maritime pines blend, was established in 1999 and is found in Donoratico, very close to the sea.

31 **The cypresses in Bolgheri**
"The cypresses that in Bolgheri, tall and straight, // Go from San Guido in a double row, // As if in a race, giant youths, // Leaped towards me and looked at me..."
(Giosuè Carducci, in front of San Guido, 1885)

32 **The cypresses in San Gimignano**
Above the hills and cypresses the profile of San Gimignano rises, perhaps the most famous village in Tuscany. Its fame is due primarily to the towers. In medieval times, there were 72; today, 14 remain.The oldest is the Rognosa Tower from the early 13th century, the tallest is the Grossa Tower, standing at 54 meters.

33 **Struzzi Metropolitani**
The artwork "Struzzi Metropolitani" by Yu Zhaoyang is found on the municipal road of Catignano between Pievasciata and Ponte a Bozzone and is part of the Chianti Sculpture Park. Originally, the figures looked into the windows of a skyscraper; now, they hide almost shyly behind two cypress trees: a sudden transition from metropolitan to bucolic that the two figures would certainly have appreciated.

34 **San Gimignano**
To most people, the names Ezio Auditore and Assassin's Creed may not mean much, but enthusiasts will definitely remember a landmark video game from 2009. In a fantasy-filled and inaccurate plot, the protagonist of the game, Ezio Auditore, climbs the Grossa Tower in San Gimignano before establishing his residence in a villa just outside Monteriggioni. Incredibly, the video game became so famous that it increased tourism in the area.

35 **Pazzi Chapel**
Drawing inspiration from classical Greek elements, Renaissance architecture was based on forms that, when repeated, provided balance and elegance to buildings according to the laws of recently discovered perspective. Andrea de' Pazzi, a noble family of wealthy Florentine merchants, commissioned Brunelleschi to build the family memorial chapel. The form chosen by the famous architect was the diameter of the dome, which had to be equal to the height of the walls and the width of the space: geometrically, a cube surmounted by a hemisphere. The two side wings covered with barrel vaults and the altar apse, with dimensions one-fifth of the module, were to be added later. The inspiration drew heavily from the Old Sacristy in San Lorenzo, but not in the decoration of the space entrusted to Luca della Robbia and not to Donatello, with whom Brunelleschi—advocating the superiority of architecture over sculpture and painting—had quarreled to the death. The chapel did not serve the Pazzi family for long; in 1478, the Pazzi Conspiracy shifted the balance of Renaissance Florence in favor of the Medici, eliminating almost all members of the family.

36 **Castiglione della Pescaia**
"...at the silver castle with three towers, surmounted by three crescents rising of the same". Forgetting the Pisans who built the castle, the municipal coat of arms recalls the rulers before the birth of the Grand Duchy of Tuscany: the Piccolomini—with three crescent moons—and the Aragonese—with three towers. Few remember that in the cemetery-garden of Castiglione della Pescaia, in the pine forest of Roccamare, Italo Calvino is buried. Struck by the place, he chose this Maremma seaside location as his "buen retiro" from 1972.

37 **The cypresses of San Quinto d'Orcia**
They seem to have been born as a "roccolo di caccia", a grove of trees created by hunters to attract birds and then capture them with nets. Now the cypresses of San Quirico are a true symbol of the Val d'Orcia, on par with Pienza and Bagno Vignoni. They are among the 55 monumental trees protected by the Tuscany Region.

2024 © SIME BOOKS
Toscana
First Edition
ISBN 978-88-31403-34-4

Text: Massimo Borchi
Translation: Esther Rosendahl, Carlo Irek
Design: WHAT! Design
Layout and illustration: Beatrice Martinotto
Pre-press: Fabio Mascanzoni
Photos: Massimo Borchi, Guido Cozzi

Most of the photos are available on www.simephoto.com

Publisher:
Sime srl
www.simebooks.com

Distribution:
ITALY
ATIESSE Rappresentanze
cutomerservice@simebooks.com
T. +39 091 6143954

GERMANY
Vertried für ZWEI
www.vertriebfuerzwei.de

UNITED STATES
SUNSET & VENICE, LLC
www.sunsetandvenice.com